Polk City's Early History:
Before 1900

Roxana Currie

Camp Pope
2010

Second edition, 2010

Library of Congress Control Number: 2010928229

ISBN: 978-1-929919-25-3

Camp Pope Publishing
P.O. Box 2232
Iowa City, Iowa 52244
www.camppope.com

On the cover: the elm tree in the middle of Highway 415.
Photo courtesy of Lee Harvey.

The author would like to acknowledge the encouragement
and financial support of the Polk City Chamber of
Commerce and the Big Creek Historical Society.

Thank you.

Contents

Illustrations

Contents

Preface to the Second Edition

April 11, 2010

This book is laid out in a way that is logical to me. The time before European settlement in Iowa is called "pre-historic," but life did not begin in Polk City, Iowa, when George Beebe staked out lots. Life had been abundant long before that. Life is a meta-story. In Iowa, that story begins with the land. That's what Chapter One is about.

Chapter Two contains pioneer stories, the mini-stories of families who came before the Civil War. They're incredible stories to me. What motivated them to endure the hardship they endured? I'm always looking for clues to why and how they triumphed over the adversity they faced.

The third chapter is about Leonard Brown. He's a fascinating character, one of the many I've written about that I wish I could sit down and talk to. He illustrates the pivotal point the Civil War played in American History.

Chapter Four is about the settlement of the community. Before the war, pioneers came and conquered. After the war, settlers came and incorporated. The railroad came and businesses were established. Life was much different than in the pioneer days.

Chapter Five is about the Polk City Cemetery. History is real there in the living context of the prairie the settlers conquered.

This remarkable site keeps community in perspective. The prairie is 3000 years old. The oldest tombstone is only 150.

Each of these chapters is part of what went into the making of Polk City: the prairie that made the land, the land that drew the people and the people who built the community. We have been many things. After the Native Americans left we were just a mill along Big Creek. Then some stakes were laid out and we were a town. When George Beebe decided to run his streets parallel to Big Creek instead of "straight with the world" he influenced every one of our lives!

We had high hopes; maybe the capital of the state, surely at least the county seat. But those dang politicians...moving around borders and such....

We quickly became an urban center. Oh yes, the burial vault confirms that we were. When a trip to Des Moines couldn't be made in a day, Polk City was where the rural people came to trade.

Then the railroad came—and left—left us high and dry with only a spur line so the train could back into town to pick up the cream and drop off the mail. Who were we then? And just when we were getting used to being one of a thousand little bitty towns in Iowa, Saylorville Lake was built. Who are we now?

The constant in Polk City's 150 years of history is the people. Communities are just people, going about their daily lives, relating to each other in neighborhoods and schools and churches and pizza places and bars and coffee shops, people who love and laugh and enjoy life, people whose lives are invaded by sickness and family problems and money problems, no matter who they are or when they live. It's every day life and regular people that make up the story of a community.

That reminds me of my favorite lines from Leonard Brown's poem written for the national centennial in 1876, "Auld Lang Syne."

> There were many names to mention
> There is much I have omitted
> Every man that stands before me
> Every woman, child and baby
> Everybody and their neighbors
> Should be mentioned in this story
> In this history of Big Creek.
> Let this history be continued....

A special thanks to Ed Rood, retired editor of the *Tri-County Times,* for giving me the opportunity to originally research and write Polk City stories, and for letting me reprint some of those articles in *Polk City's Early History: Before 1900.*

Chapter 1: Pre-settlement

A Look at Polk City's Roots

Reprinted from the *Tri-County Times,* June 9, 1994

Even though the Big Creek settlement began in 1846, the larger picture of European Colonization and the Western movement of the European settler is also part of our history, especially as it influenced the Native Americans.

The Ioway Indians were recorded as being here during the pre-settlement era. They are where our state's name came from. Probably they were not native to this area, but were pushed here by the advancing Europeans. Some individual Ioway probably survived, but they are one tribe that through disease and genocide ceased to exist as a people.

The Sac and Fox were moved to this area from Wisconsin after siding with the French in a conflict in the 1730s. They were forced to cede land in 1804 and again in 1824. Finally they made a last stand effort to keep what remained of their home of a hundred years in the spring of 1832 under Chief Blackhawk. After their defeat, the 150 survivors of Blackhawk's band were forced to give up the eastern quarter of Iowa effective 1837. Polk County was within the remaining Sac and Fox reservation until the title transferred by treaty to the U. S. Government Oct. 11, 1845.

To facilitate the removal of the Indians, in the spring of 1835 Colonel Stephen Kearny was instructed to "proceed up the Des Moines River to the Raccoon Fork...for the purpose of examining that vicinity as a suitable place for a military post." Excerpts from his and several of his company's diaries were reprinted in the January 1963, *Palimpsest,* which is the source of the following.

Kearny's soldiers were a company specializing in exploration—Dragoons. They began the eleven hundred-mile march on June 7, 1835. At "Keokuk's Town" near Agency, Iowa, several Native Americans joined them, and Frank Labashure was their interpreter. Rain hampered their efforts. One member of the expedition described the weather as a "succession of rains, blows, and chills: and if the sun happens to shine, it does so gloomily, as if boding a coming storm. The whole country becomes saturated with water; the low lands are overflowed; the streams are swollen; and locomotion is rendered difficult except by water."

Indeed they were marching along the watershed dividing the Skunk and Des Moines rivers. Even if they camped on dry ground, a storm often came up in the night. But by they time they were as far north as the present site of Oskaloosa the weather had changed. They marched through prairies "covered with strawberries" so abundant "as to make the whole track red for miles." They were marching about 15 miles per day, and feasted on strawberries for many weeks. Good fortune smiled doubly upon them as at the same time, "one of our beeves became a milker." Strawberries and cream!

There was abundant game: turkey, grouse, ducks, prairie chickens, deer and an occasional bear or buffalo. Fish abounded in every stream. The soldiers' pork had run out but they had plenty of food. Colonel Kearny realized he was further north than the Raccoon Fork of the Des Moines, so on June 22nd he turned northeastward toward Wabasha's village.

"Not far from the head of Skunk (Chicaqua) river, in the midst of an ocean of fine native grass, such as only Iowa produces," wrote Lieutenant Albert M. Lea, "we encountered a small herd of buffalo, to which many of us gave chase." Lea was excited about his first glimpse of "the lordly beast in his home." That night not only buffalo were in abundance; when Lea's tent was pitched four rattlers were killed inside it. Fortunately, Lea was fascinated by the native fauna. He pressed a huge mosquito in his journal and kept it for years as "a specimen of the luxuriant growth of the Plaines."

By the Fourth of July they had crossed into Minnesota, and three days later they reached Wabasha's village near where Winona is now located. They stayed twelve days, then turned back south. On July 21, they crossed a branch of the "Iway", perhaps the Cedar River, and suddenly found their way blocked by a long lake. Finally surrounding the lake, they turned southward and marched for 8 days straight, not sure where they were, except that it was a beautiful place. "During this season the appearance of the country is gay and beautiful, being clothed in grass, foliage, and flowers." August 2nd they hit the Des Moines and spent six hours crossing it by raft. The next day they crossed again further south by means of a ford. They continued down the west bank, crossing the Lizard, Bluff, Beaver, and other creeks. Finally they pitched their tents at the Raccoon Fork in a "grassy and spongy meadow with a bubbling spring."

The next day Kearny explored the area. The Des Moines was 120 yards wide, but easily crossed because it was so shallow. There was an abundance of timber, but Kearny did not recommend building a fort there. William Peterson explains his reasoning in the *Palimpsest*. "Transportation of military stores on large boats was extremely uncertain; the Sacs and Sioux were at peace and needed no such barrier; the site at the upper fork of the Des Moines was much more practicable; and the Indians themselves opposed the erection of a post on the Raccoon River 'giving as one of their objections, that the Whites would drive off the little game remaining."

But as we know, the fort was built at the fork of the Des Moines and Raccoon Rivers and was named Fort Des Moines. The advance of settlers would not be stopped. The lands were surveyed and opened for settlement: the Half-breed Tract in 1824, the Black Hawk Purchase in 1832 and '37, and the Sac and Fox Cessation of 1842. On October 10, 1845, the drama of the uprooted and decimated Native Americans shoved ever westward was enacted yet once more. At midnight the settlers staked their claims by the light of burning Native's wickiups, accompanied by the sounds of gunshots and wild celebration.

The first white settlers who came to Big Creek in '45 and '46 were squatters buying and selling claims, including Barlow, Beebe, Canfield, Elliott, Howard, Lamb, McClain, Marts, Meachan, Mitchell, Newcomer, Saylor, Stutzman, and Van Dorn. The land could not be purchased until it was surveyed— the fall of 1848 it was finally for sale by the government.

The land was Iowa, and it proved to be rich and productive—despite the early speculation that land which couldn't grow trees wouldn't produce crops, either. It was a chance at a new life for only $1.25 per acre.

Within a space of 40 years, from 1835–1875, government troops had explored the land, a fort had been established and vacated, the land was surveyed and sold, and the American pioneer—farmers, businessmen, railroaders and speculators—laid the foundation for a new era of Iowa history.

Central Iowa's Changing Waterways
Reprinted from the *Tri-County Times,* Aug. 8, 1996

Iowans are ever bent on conquering the land and water. Some even have the audacity of the contractor who has recently razed the trees bordering a sleepy little stream, straightened it, dumped limestone rocks along its banks, and named his development "Bubbling Brook"!

When Isaac Galland called to the *Iowa Emigrant* in 1840, he described some of the larger waterways in the state. We've all read of the Mighty Mississippi, though none of us can imagine it. Galland stretches our imagination further when he describes the fertile soil and abundant timber of the Skunk River, racing 150 yards wide through its winding channel. The Missouri was called by the Sauk and Fox the River of Vortexes, or Whirlpools.

Our own Des Moines River was described by Galland as averaging 300 yards in width. "Its waters are transparent, and its current swift and shallow; it abounds in streams and springs of excellent water are in many places found in great profusion along its shores." In stark contrast, the DNR's *Iowa Fish and Fishing,* 1987 edition, describes the Des Moines as a "slow-flowing stream. During high water periods it carries a heavy load of silt. Through much of its course, the channel consists of drift sand and large mud bars are common."

The changing of Iowa's waterways was almost an instant result of European settlement. The Swamp Act passed by the US Congress in 1850 affected 15,000 acres in Polk County. These acres became the property of the county in 1855. The proceeds of the sale of swamplands had to be used to drain them. By 1862 all the lands were disposed of and as Dixon's *Centennial History of Polk County* boasted in 1880, "Polk County realized quite a large amount of revenue. And the swamplands became

13

the property of private individuals and a large proportion of them have become the most desirable and productive land in the county."

Netti Sanford's *Early Sketches of Polk County, Iowa* (published 1874), captures the settlers' vision. "Horseshoe Lake was drained off," Sanford says, "much to the disgust of the wild geese and brandts, in the spring of 1859, and where frog ponds and dismal hollows disfigured the surface, gardens and door yards bloomed with shrubbery and flowers."

The early milling industry in less than 15 years resulted in more than 1,000 dams being built on the smaller creeks and rivers of Iowa. Leland Sage's *A History of Iowa* states, "The dam need not be high or the stream large. A head of 3 or 4 feet would suffice." Even this seemingly minor slowing down of the waterway changed the character of the creek bottom, the temperature of the water, and the vegetation. One of the first activities of the State Fish Commission in 1874 was to promote the construction of Fish Passageways over the many dams to allow for seasonal migration of several threatened fish species *(Iowa Fish and Fishing)*. This controversial conservation effort resulted in a series of "Dam Elegies" written as editorials pro and con in newspapers. As one poet quipped, "Music hath charms," 'tis said, "to soothe the savage beast;" But for putting in a 'Fishway' 'portry' [poetry] works the best."

Seth Meek made the first systematic effort to survey the state's fish in the 1880s. A short 34 years after the very first settlers, in 1890 he wrote: "I have been informed that many streams, formerly deep and narrow, and abounding in pickerel, bass, and catfishes, have since grown wide and shallow, while the volume of water in them varies greatly in the different seasons, and they are inhabited only by bullheads, suckers, and a few minnows. The soil, since loosed with the plow, is much more easily washed into the streams than when it was covered with native sod. Thus the water in these streams is muddier than formerly; in wet weather deeper, in dry weather more shallow. These are a probable cause for a diminution of some of the food fishes." *(Iowa Fish and Fishing)* The DNR publication goes on to conclude the greatest declines have been those with habitat requirements for clearer, cooler, or more vegetated waters. Indeed, early settler reports of trout fishing at Iowa Falls and other points in Iowa are met with disbelief today, when the trout in even our Northeastern streams are stocked at a ready to catch size.

Reeve Bailey, writing 60 years after Meek in an earlier edition of *Iowa Fish and Fishing,* suggested it was doubtful "whether any other state has experienced such extensive reduction in its original fish fauna". Forty years after Bailey, 69% of the animals cited in the 1989 "Endangered or Threatened Plant and Animal Species" of the Iowa Code are related to our waterways; fish, reptiles and amphibians, snails and clams.

Bruce Menzel writes in the currant edition, "During the past century, most of the Des Moines Lobe has been converted from wet prairie to one of the most intensively cropped agricultural tracts in the country. Of an estimated 6 million acres of wetlands existing at the time of settlement, less than 30,000 remain. More than 1/2 of the lakes have been drained through a network of ditches and straightened streams." Our average 31" of rainfall, which in the past lounged in sloughs and potholes long enough to renew our waters and vegetation, now race out of the state much too quickly. With the changes thrust upon the Iowa waterways in the past hundred years, it's no wonder those century floods are inundating the land so frequently today.

A Dam Elegy—Tacitus Hussey

From *A History of Early Des Moines*

Said the Pickerel to the Catfish:
"I heard rare news today;
That the dam down here at Bonaparte
Will have a good fish-way!
I can't be pious here below;
For staying where I am
I bump against the structure
And invariably say 'Dam!"
Then the game fish fell to shouting
At the good news they had heard-
The Catfish opened wide his mouth,
But never gasped a word!
Said the Quillback to the Sucker:
"I hate to be confined
To this one spot forever-
I'm afraid I'll lose my mind;
This dam roaring makes my head ache."
"Say, look here," said the Bass:
"Ask the Fish and Game Committees
To give us all a pass!"
Then the Quillback took the bandage
From off his aching head-
"You're a scaly lot of fellows!"
The big-mouthed Catfish said.
Said the Salmon the Goggle Eye
"When this fish-way is in place,
I'll strike out for headquarters
At a good two-forty pace!
The dam roaring and head-thumping
Will ne'er again be mine-

And perhaps our friends, the fishermen,
Will be dropping us a line!"
Then the game fish burst out laughing,
Nodding each expectant head-
"Meeks will roar much louder than the dam!"
The grinning Catfish said.
Said the Mullet to the Catfish:
"I've just heard something new;
That the Fish Clubs and Game Warden
Have been making game of you;
That the 'Sucker Tribe' you've shaken
And you're classed with Pike and Bass!"
Then the smiling Catfish: "Yes,
I'm swimming in that class!"
Then the Eel began to grumble
About this new-found preference-
"Well, a big mouth", said the Mullet,
"Often stands in stead of sense!"
When the fish-way had been finished,
And the Meeks had shed their tears,
There was the biggest "Fish Convention"
That had been held there for years!
With their loins now firmly girded,
And in each fin a staff,
They prepared to give "Old Bonaparte"
The "Grand Razzle-Dazzle" laugh!
As they climbed the road to freedom
Everybody had to smile,
For the glad flip-flapping of their tails
Could be heard for half a mile!

Waukonsa

Reprinted from the *Tri-County Times*, March 9, 1989

Polk City's oral history includes persistent reference to the Native American village, Waukonsa. Netti Sanford confirms its existence in her book *Early Sketches of Polk County, Iowa*, printed in 1874. "Waukonsa was an Indian village whose original site is the northeastern part of Polk City. There were a good many wykyups left by the Sac that were used by the settlers. Alexander Swim fixed up his cabin with the Indian household remains, moved his family into the domicile in 1847, and placed his name amoung the earliest settlers of Madison Township."

There are many such references to Swim using the poles from the village. It was evidently recently deserted, and its name—spelled any way you want it to be—was Waukonsa.

That seems to be all that's known about the village, though. The original surveyor records and maps make no mention of a village, even though it would have been very near a township line where they would have been exploring. When Polk City's boundary expanded west of Booth Street, the area was called the Waukonsa addition.

Kathy Gourley did research for the Historic Preservation Office of the Iowa State Historical Society to determine the sites of the Raccoon River Indian Agency and the Sac and Fox towns it served. She has been able to use oral tradition and official correspondence to pinpoint many of those towns along the Des Moines. Her research has not found that any Sac town was this far north in 1845. Ms. Gourley speculated it might have been the home of some of the bands that didn't use the agency or recognize the government's authority over them.

Another idea is that the town was a village of the Sioux. Waukonsa is the name of a Sioux Indian boy who was a close friend of a trader located in the Fort Dodge area. His story is in several histories. The name may also indicate some kind of spiritual site, Waukon being Sioux for Spirit. Although the word is clearly Sioux in origin, they were basically in Minnesota and the Dakotas and their records are there. Little investigation of their existence in Iowa has been done aside from the much-publicized Spirit Lake Massacre.

If the town was Sioux, it would explain why there are no references in the Sac and Fox Agency records. But the Sioux lived a nomadic lifestyle and didn't build permanent villages. They would have taken everything, including the poles of their houses, with them. They wouldn't have left enough behind for early white settlers to build a house out of. If the Sioux left their village behind, it raises more questions about why the town was abandoned.

Tim Morton of Polk City has an ongoing interest in native America history. He says that Waukonsa "is just a drop in the bucket." He has collected many artifacts in the Polk City area, some dating back to the end of the ice age. Area farmers are knowledgeable about Indian artifacts, several having "a box of arrowheads" from the fields they have plowed over the years.

Jerome Thompson of the State Historical Society has the same opinion as Morton. Polk City probably has "several village sites, especially pre-historic ones."

The Saylorville Recreation Area is registered as a Nation Historic Site because of the number of pre-historic sites, including burial mounds and village sites. Dr. David Gradwohl of Iowa State University did much of the preliminary survey of the lake area, but did no investigation in Polk City proper. He has heard of Waukonsa, though, and has no doubt of the accuracy of the oral tradition. In his opinion, the best way to find the village site and specifics now is to listen to the people of Polk City. What do they find when they build a garage or dig a basement or plow their gardens? Those are the clues that could pinpoint what and where Waukonsa was. It's difficult to find a historic Indian village though—much harder than finding a pre-historic one. By 1840, (in fact, by 1740) the things Native Americans had in their towns were very similar to the things found in white settlements. Iron pots were over their cooking fires. European rifles killed their game. The things they still made themselves— wooden utensils, blankets, clothing—are not things that keep. The best clue to an historic Indian village is an abundance of glass beads.

Waukonsa may always remain a mystery, but one thing is certain. The Des Moines River Valley was populated by Native Americans millennia before Europeans dreamed of a New World to conquer. The beautiful wooded hilltop between Big Creek and the Des Moines River, with its abundant wildlife, water, and other resources, appealed to the Native Americans for the same reason it attracted the first white settlers venturing up the Des Moines in 1846.

Spring, 1846

Spring, 1846—it's a spring like central Iowa will never see again. Ice in shallow sloughs and swamps slowly melts, making a continuous watery highway for multitudes of migrating water birds. The morning and evening calls of the birds fill the air.

The Des Moines River is wide and meandering. Its timber belt averages 5 miles wide. Mighty oaks are truly mighty, White Oaks averaging 25 inches diameter, Burr Oaks 24-30", Red Oaks, 15-20". There are a variety of nut and berry trees. Elms are abundant, Red, White, and Corky Elm, from 10 to 30" in diameter. Maple and Ash flourish. The river species add diversity of textures and colors, giant Cottonwoods, wispy Willows, and Birch. Pre-settlement Central Iowa Forests hug the life-giving waterways.

Big Creek has its own small timber belt. Less impacted by spring flooding than the Des Moines, the creek banks are home to the Choke Cherry, Wild Plum, Gooseberry, Currant, Witch Hazel, Grape, Dogwood, Elderberry, Honeysuckle... dozens of smaller trees and bushes. This is the bountiful land awaiting the pioneer.

But neither the timber nor the prairie had come to life when Samuel Hays and his family, including his brother John, braved the earliest spring weather to arrive in March of 1846. There were few neighbors to greet them. Evan Harris was here, and a man named Shipman lived in a log cabin about a mile and a half northwest of where the Hays settled.

The Hays brothers weren't satisfied with their land along Big Creek, and in May of '46, they sold the claim to George Beebe. Sam apparently stayed in this area. He and his daughter were both buried at the Polk City Cemetery in 1850, possibly victims of some early epidemic. John rented land from John Saylor for two years and married Martha Saylor in '48. They later moved to Des Moines, where he was an early sheriff. In 1876 John Hays talked about that first summer in Polk County for Dixon's centennial book. "Aside from the garrison buildings, which extended for some distance along the banks of both rivers, the improvements at the Fort were few and insignificant. What is now called East Des Moines was divided into farms, and the greater part of the site of the present city was covered with dense and primitive thickets of hazel bushes." Dixon continues, "Mr. Hays established himself in a rude log cabin, with but one room in it, located on Second Street, between Walnut and Locust. The house is still standing, [in 1876] as a memento and memorial of a past age." (*Centennial History of Polk County, Iowa*, Mrs. J. M. Dixon, Des Moines, 1876)

In May the settlers came in earnest. Besides George Beebe,

Rev. Marts, Andrew Grosclose, J. M. Marts, William Herbert, Andrew Messersmith, Peter Miller, D. B. Spaulding, Byroms, Cal Burt, Conrad Stutzman, Samuel Hunt, and the John Crabtree family were some of the earliest. Conflicting records make it difficult to set exact dates for people arriving before 1848.

Messersmiths were sutlers to the new fort established in Northwest Iowa, Fort Dodge.

Grosclose, Stutzman, and Beebe erected mills along Big Creek. The mills also served as the social center of the day. Mrs. Stutzman was noted to be a hospitable woman, welcoming travelers to "stop off" at her home. But the mills that were indispensable in '46 were all but obsolete by the time the flood of 1851 washed them away. Grosclose moved on up the river where mill power was still needed in less established areas. Stutzmans moved to Des Moines and ran a successful hotel. George Beebe built a dry goods store and sold off lots, founding the town of Polk City.

Alexander Swim operated the first mill in Polk City that spring; a horse powered mill that ground corn into cornmeal for many years. Some of our older residents remember taking corn to Swim's mill, west of Booth Street.

People came west for milling or soldiering or scouting or business, but most came for land. At $1.25 an acre, a dream was for sale. Swim used the remains of Waukonsa to build the cabin on his farm, which included the land where the nursing home now stands on Washington St. The Hunt family stayed on the west side of the river, later welcoming the Murrays and Nicholsons. Josiah Hopkins settled his family in a grove west of Polk City. L. M. Small was in that same area. Cal Burt lost his young wife in the new land as he settled to the north on Wolf Creek.

The timber belts were quickly settled. Cabins, barns, buildings, fences, all were built from trees on the claim. Then acres of land were grubbed and the trees just burned to create tillable land, as the pioneer couldn't yet survive far enough from the life-giving creeks and rivers to farm the vast prairies.

Sixteen counties, including Polk, filled up rapidly in 1846. The Union Historical Company's *The History of Polk County, Iowa*, says of the Big Creek Settlement, "This was a most favorite region of the country, and not only did the western bound emigrants flock in there in large numbers, but they made their mark. The influence of this settlement was felt in the social, political and industrial affairs of the county, and it plays a most important part in the history of the county." The dream of land and a new life; many found it right here 150 years ago.

Chapter 2: Before the War

George Beebe—Polk City's Founder

Reprinted from the *Tri-County Times,* March 30, 1989

The Beebe family was among the earliest settlers in Polk County. Originally from New York, George and Hester were in Missouri during the persecution of the 1830s and were themselves the victims of several beatings and whippings according to their descendant, Vearis Lisenbee. They started west from Nauvoo, Illinois as part of a Mormon wagon train headed for Utah in early 1846. They arrived in central Iowa in May, spending the night at Martin Tucker's "Hotel" in a garrison building at the Fort. For unknown reasons, they decided to go up the river and "stake claim" in Iowa instead of Utah.

John and Samuel Hays had come to the present site of Polk City earlier that spring, but "circumstances not necessary to narrate here induced them to move the same season to Saylor's Grove, after having disposed of their possessions to George Beebe, one of the patriarchs of Madison Township" (Dixon's *Centennial History of Polk County, Iowa)*. In November of 1848 he bought two half sections of land at the government price of $1.25 per acre.

Beebe's home is recorded as being one of true pioneer hospitality. Because of its place in the country's history, several tales have been recorded about it. The cabin reportedly was built without "chinkin" and the wolves used to stick their noses in through the cracks. When it stormed, "vigorous sweeping was necessary to prevent putting out the fire on the hearth." (Andrews: *Pioneers of Polk County.)*

In the summer, mosquitoes were so bad no one could cross the river to visit the Beebe's without wearing coat, mittens, and a veil. Mrs. Beebe wrapped up the same way to sit in her doorway in the summer, or the plague would quickly leave her hands a bloody mess.

A veil was also used over a dry goods box to "bolt the flour" as it was ground too coarsely for cakes. In spite of all inconveniences, the Beebes hosted picnics, sledding parties, quilting bees, church and government meetings as the settlement grew.

Reason and Robert Howard came in 1849. Netti Sanford's *Early Sketches of Polk County, Iowa* says: "When they got discouraged a visit to the Beebes' cabin was in order, and the Esquire would comfort them be telling old pioneer stories of three years before."

In May of 1850 Beebe plotted the town of Polk City on part of his land. "There was no competing town nearer than the Fort and he at once set in motion plans for a trading center. He built a much-needed mill on Big Creek, opened a general merchandise store, sold lots, and invited people to come. And they did... It was a rival of the Fort for State Capitol." (Andrews: *Pioneers of Polk County)*

Mrs. Anna Turley of Des Moines was one of the last survivors of the wagon train Beebes traveled with. In 1938 she wrote: "They stopped in Iowa instead of going to the Salt Lake Valley with the rest of the Mormons. Mr. Beebe was a successful farmer and his home was always a refuge and a stopping place for the Mormon elders traveling through Iowa. They had to walk so much during the olden days that they were always glad to get to the Beebe's home to repair their clothing and rest..."

"Mrs. Beebe wanted to go west and live with the rest of the Latter Day Saints, but her husband had such a good business with the flouring mills that he did not want to leave. On one of her visits to Salt Lake City, she went to Brigham Young and said, 'What do I do now? I want to live here and Mr. Beebe has so much business he doesn't want to leave Iowa.' Brigham Young answered her, "you go to your husband and you will come back here to the West to lay your bones.'"

The last record we have of George Beebe is his vote on the incorporation of Polk City on March 25, 1875. Some time before 1880 they did go west to Provo, Utah. They left behind two landmarks in the community.

One is the cemetery on East Broadway, which was fenced and marked as a historic site as part of Polk City's Centennial celebration in 1975. The cemetery has four stones currently in

The Beebe Cemetery, east of the Square in Polk City. Photo by Roxana Currie.

26

place, yet the CCC survey records from the 1930s indicate at least six of George and Hester Beebe's children were buried there. The following is taken from a clipping for the Historical Department of the Latter Day Saints in Salt Lake City, Utah, and adds another name and date to the cemetery records. It is originally from the *Des Moines Evening News,* December 6, 1869. "We (Brother Stephen C. Perry and four other elders) are stopping at our brother George Beebee's [*sic*] at Polk City, 15 miles north of Des Moines. We held our regular fast meeting at his house on Thursday last, most particularly on account of Brother Beebee's son, Alvaro, who has been paralyzed in his entire body, so that he has been as helpless as a child for three months."

The fast meetings as described in the narrative involve not eating for a day, then washing and anointing the sick young man. A news item of January 5, 1870, notes: "brother Stevenson writes from Polk City on the 25th ... the day before he and brother Pratt attended the funeral of Brother Alvaro Beebe, who died on the 23rd at Polk City. The deceased was only 19 years, 7 months, and 20 days old; and up to last June was a youth of great promise." The article elaborates on the illness of Alvaro, noting also that he was 6' 7" tall. Today no stone marks Alvaro's grave.

Three daughters of George and Hester Beebe were also buried here during the family's 30-year stay. Georgianna died at only 20 days, with no date visible on her stone. Ozanna was born Oct. 15, 1860, and died November 5, 1874. Martha was born July 7, 1846, (two months after the family decided to stop in Polk City rather than continue on to Utah) and died February 18, 1848.

The other landmark they left us is the City Square. Polk City Square has been the center of community activity for 150 years. When the town was platted, the Beebes donated the square to

An early view of Polk City's Town Square.
Photo courtesy of Big Creek Historical Society.

the community, stipulating that it would always remain a park, or revert to the Beebe family.

One of the Beebe children, David, was a schoolteacher for one winter in Polk City and operated a steam engine here, sometime before 1875. He and his brothers established a lumber company and store in Provo after the family emigrated.

Cal Burt—Early Polk City Settler
Reprinted from the *Tri-County Times,* Nov. 2, 1989

Calvin Burt, know as C. M. in the history books and Cal to his friends and family, was born in St. Lawrence County, New York on June 23, 1818. His son, James Wilson Burt (b. 1868) wrote a family history, which has been donated to the Polk City Community Library by Janet Halstead of Huntington Beach, California. Janet is Cal's great-granddaughter. The family history contains many stories of pioneer life.

As a young man, Cal Burt migrated to Wisconsin where he worked getting out timber and floating it down the Wisconsin and Mississippi Rivers. He often told his children about "birling" logs to see who could stay on them the longest while spinning in the water. It was while floating logs to Dubuque that Burt met his sweetheart, Elizabeth. Soon he gave up logging in favor of homesteading. He and Elizabeth were married in 1844 and later went to St. Joseph, Missouri, intending to settle in Oregon. "But they changed their minds and moved to Polk City," James Burt wrote, "which was the most prosperous place in central Iowa."

Elizabeth's death in June of 1847 is recorded in several Polk County history books as the first settler's death in Madison Township. It is dramatically picture in Leonard Brown's Centennial Poem, "Auld Lang Syne."

Calvin Burt with his companion,
Anchored here and built their cabin.
But, alas! It soon was lonely
The companion of his bosom
Soon was carried in her coffin,
From the door of that one cabin—
The first funeral attended—
The first grave dug of the pale-face
In the neighborhood of Big Creek.
Let me give a panorama
Of the funeral procession,
Moving forward to the grave-yard;
Several wagons I have counted
Drawn by oxen and by horses—
For the people then were friendly-
For they then were truly neighbors
Felt the sympathy of children-

For the griefs of one another,
There were Uncle Jacob Van Dorn,
William, Abner, George and Isaac...

Elizabeth's death left Cal with a two-year-old son, and the next year he found a mother for the little boy in Mary Crabtree. The Crabtree genealogy tells us their marriage is the first recorded in Polk County, that is, the first after records began to be kept. That was February 1, 1848.

Burt purchased a farm on Wolf Creek north of Polk City, but evidently wanted more timber. He sold that place and bought land along Big Creek and built a log house. He told the children of weather so cold that he would sit with his back to the fireplace to write, and even though he could hardly stand the heat on his back, the ink would freeze in his pen.

In that house, four more children were born and one died. Mary Crabtree Burt also died in March of 1858.

Now Burt was twice widowed with four children, a thirteen year old boy, 7 year-old twins, and three year old Henry. But he found a willing partner in Mary Wilson and they were married that fall. Mary was only 20 years old.

Despite her youth and heavy responsibilities, her son James wrote she was

a whiz to get things done. She was like the nursery rhyme. "She could bake a cherry pie quick as a cat could wink its eye" (nearly). But the crust was as thin as paper and as flaky as you please. There were pies every day, besides doughnuts and cookies on hand all the time. The doughnuts were cut in strips and swift twists made them into a figure eight. In a half hour, there would be a hat full cooked. Every morning, there were fried potatoes with bacon or ham with gravy. For dinner, as it was called in the middle of the day, there was a big meal with boiled potatoes, fried meat and gravy. But in the evening, the supper was warmed over stuff. She had the quaintest cook stove, about two feet square and an oven that seemed more like

C. M. Burt and his third wife, Mary E. Wilson Burt. Photo courtesy of Janet Halstead-Sinclair.

a doll stove. The front had a grate and a door that could be swung back where the bread was toasted and the sweet corn roasted.

Nothing was ever thrown away. All merchandise had to be laboriously hauled from Keokuk up the Des Moines River. Cal made many of those supply trips himself, even in the middle of winter.

Cal's brother, Darius, visited Polk City in the early 1850s. This extended visit ended in tragedy when Darius died during an epidemic in 1855.

In 1862 Burt joined the Union Army, as did Mary's brother Clark. In 1863 Clark died and 18 year-old George enlisted. Mary had the care of three stepchildren and two babies, along with running the farm and cooking for the hired men. She saved enough money during the war to request better quarters for her growing family. When Cal came home they left the log house and he built her a new one, which still stands at the west end of Hug Drive. Cal got out timber for the house with his team, Jim and Frank. He would take the team out and hang the line on the hames, throw a chain around a log and drive or back them with a "get up" or "back," never touching the lines in the process. Some of the logs had to be hauled to Des Moines to be made into finished lumber for the floors.

The house is in the "Salt Box" style common to the era—two rooms 14' square on each floor of a two-story house with

31

a roof extended over a long kitchen and bedroom in the back. After the house was built, Mary finally got a bigger stove.

Burt had little education, but he "was never ignorant because like Abe Lincoln, he thoroughly knew his Bible." He was a class leader and led the singing at the Methodist Church. He was on the Board of Trustees for the Township, School Board and City Council at Polk City. He could discuss current events and politics with anyone. His grandfather fought in the Revolutionary War and Cal was a very patriotic man. State and County Republicans kept him in cigars. (According to his son, he always kept his cigar pointed at the sky: it never drooped!) His knowledge of history and geography was very complete.

He came West with the very first wave of emigrants and endured the hardships of that time. His third wife, Mary, died in 1888. By the time of his own death in 1891, Cal had buried two brothers, three wives and six children at the Polk City cemetery. Surely there's no better picture of the price our early settlers paid to establish our state and our community.

James Wilson

Father Wilson was born in Ireland St. Patrick's Day, 1805. He was raised on a farm there and farmed until he left home August 13, 1826, to try life in the new land. He landed in Quebec, then went to Vermont, where he married Miranda Nash in 1830. They went back to Canada, then to Ohio in '33 where he operated a tannery and shoe business.

James Wilson was Methodist, and "being a good talker, and found to be well versed in the Bible...attracted the attention of the church officials," according to a family historian. He was first given an exhorter's license. The exhorters were the backbone of the Methodist paradigm. They were uneducated, but devoted to God and to the saving of lost souls. Later he was given a preacher's license, but he didn't join the conference and take a circuit immediately. He didn't want to be sent from place to place, "particularly as Grandfather lived with us and our family was large." He eventually did take a circuit in Indiana, then another back in Ohio. In 1855 or '56 he came to Polk City with his nearly grown family and his preaching credentials. (As they were on the way, someone asked where they were headed, then informed the family "that was where the women quarreled so much.")

A family story from that time tells of an ox running away with the wagon as they were coming down a long hill. But the teammate refused to run and was dragged with his knees braced all the way down the hill. The minister often "thanked the Lord for the bravery of an ox."

The children were taught to be thankful. Once when supplies were low supper consisted of boiled potatoes "in jackets." Someone complained, but big brother Robert said, "We ought to feel sorry for the poor folks that do not have salt for their potatoes." The poor meals were as blessed as the good ones, and morning and evening bible reading and prayers were never neglected in the Wilson household.

James Wilson was also a strict observer of the Sabbath. He often cobbled shoes late on Saturday night, then just before midnight sharpened his razor so as to not defile the Sabbath by shaving his beard, which was "more like spikes of steel wire to the touch than anything else" according to his grandson.

Before the war, anti-slavery agitation caused a division in the Methodist Episcopal Church, and Father Wilson changed his affiliation to Brethren. The Brethren made slavery and membership in secret orders tests of membership. Our Centennial Poem written by Leonard Brown summarizes several of the pioneer preachers with the line, "Friends of God and man and freedom, (But cold shoulder to Free Masons)."

One Sunday in December of 1881 the 75 year-old Father Wilson preached the whole day, his last engagement 50 miles from home. He returned to "sup" with Mary's family and spent the evening telling them of the progress of his work. That night he had a stroke and he lived only a week longer.

Brown's Centennial Poem eulogizes James Wilson with these words:

> Practiced teacher—honored father—
> Through a long life he had labored
> As a kind and loved instructor,
> Doing good to all, as Christ did;
> He has gone to meet his Master—
> Meet the Master whom he followed,
> Doing good to all as Christ did.

Mary Wilson Burt

Mary Wilson Burt was a pioneer woman, born to a family of Scotch immigrants. Mary did not have a "traditional" up-bringing in the James Wilson household, only the tradition of being committed to a work which needed to be done.

Mary was 20 when she married Cal Burt, a prominent Polk City resident. He was a forty-year-old farmer, very much involved in civic affairs, and twice widowed with four children, the oldest of whom was 13. A marriage of romance, or convenience, we might wonder? No matter, it was a marriage with much to do. Mary set out to make a happy home for her family, and from the reminiscence of her son, James Wilson Burt, she worked very hard at it, yet had her rules. The children could have all the milk or water they wanted, but neither coffee nor

34

tea, and the butter was watched with hawk eyes to see that it was not spread too thickly. "Jim, are you eating bread and butter or butter and bread?"

Mary's son, Walter, learned to read when he was three, and was ready for the second reader at four. Mary took the little boy shopping and asked for the second reader. The merchant put the book on the counter where Mary had sat Walter, and he immediately began to examine his prize. The merchant grabbed it with an angry word, to which Mary replied, "He thought he should be allowed to look at his own book." The merchant didn't believe it, so Walter read for him, and was rewarded (sheepishly, one would assume) with the best knife in the store.

In 1862 her husband went to war, leaving Mary with six children, one of them epileptic. The baby died before he returned home.

Mary was busy during those three war years. Besides the children and the homemaking, she now supervised the hired men. Her first winter of running the farm, '62–'63, was a blustery one in Polk County, the time of the big snow lasting three days. Yet she found time to write a long poem about the storm, and evidently handled the stress by weaving, for there were several years' worth of extra blankets by the war's end. Mary bore her tenth child five days after her father died. "That is the strenuous life lived by the women of 70 years ago," her son James wrote in his tribute. She raised fourteen children with all the teaching, nurturing, and physical chores that are part of that job. She provided a home for her father. She was a trustworthy partner for her husband, literally holding down the fort while he was doing what needed to be done on the Southern battlefields, and always feeding the hired hands and special crews the farm required."

In our day, some categorize women as farm women, working women, career women, homemakers, full-time mothers, etc. Our rural heritage defined women's roles by simply posing the question, "What needs to be done?"

Crabtree Family Had Big Effect
Reprinted from the *Tri-County Times*, December 19, 1994

Epitaphs carved on graves of John and Mary Crabtree.
> *Servant of God, well done.*
> *Thy glorious journey past.*
> *The battle fought the victory won*
> *And thou art crowned at last.*
Polk City, Iowa

> *Her children rise up and call her blessed.*
Indianola, Ne.

To You Pioneers
by Edna Alberta Crabtree

In life together young at heart
In death their graves are miles apart.
In life to each a loving mate
In death each grave a different state.
Alone may each silently rest
Alone each by the Saviour blest.
Alone where the wild winds play
Alone? No! Together and just away.
To you Pioneers who paved the way.
Your roof sky of blue
Your bed of straw or hay,
You journeyed far, o'er ocean hill and brook
To bring us close within this book.

John Crabtree was born in the "Great House" at Midgeley, Yorkshire County, England, on February 18, 1794. Both John and his father were among the fortunate educated of that era, and were both active in the official business of Midgeley township and the church. John was unaware when he left that life behind him that he was destined to be the father and grandfather of many of the business and community leaders of a small but prominent community across the ocean and thousands of miles from home, Polk City, Iowa. He came to America in 1825 with three sons, John, Matthew, and James. Other children were born to he and his wife, Mary Scott, after they settled in Ohio, but the three oldest boys longed to go west.

John Crabtree Jr.

Their firstborn, John Jr., was born in 1818. His father, John, had been active in bringing Methodism to Midgeley. Now both together became an establishing force in the Baptist Church in Newark, Ohio, working with pioneer missionary, John Fry, the first to bring Baptist doctrine to Ohio.

John Jr. came to Polk City in 1846 with his parents. His father bought nearly a section of land; John Jr. bought 1/2 section. According to the 1856 census, John Jr.'s farm consisted of:

> 8 acres improved land,
> 9 acres unimproved
> 5 acres wheat, yielding 80 bushels
> 3 acres oats, yielding 100
> 10 acres corn, yielding 400 bushels.
> potatoes yielding 50 bushels.
> 5 hogs

In 1848 he helped establish a Methodist Church in this community with 12 members. A frame building was erected in 1866, after the war on the corner of 2nd and Van Dorn.

Matthew Crabtree

Matthew Crabtree was born in 1819 in England. He was seven when the family came to Ohio. In 1847 he, his wife, Susannah, and daughter Mary Ann followed his father and brother to Polk City.

Matthew had been a wagon maker in Ohio, and he established and operated a wagon shop in Polk City until he enlisted in the Civil War.

After the war, he engaged in agriculture, but remained active in city government, serving as city marshal in 1879.

James Crabtree

James was born in 1825 and was only an infant when the family came to America. He brought his wife, small son and infant daughter to Polk City in 1848, the third son to emigrate over a period of 3 years.

In 1888, James purchased property from Nathaniel and Mary Bishop, lots 1, 2, 3 & 4, Block 6 O.P. He had a wagon shop there and also hewed both lath and shingles. It is unclear whether this is the same location as Matthew's earlier shop. He also was involved in city government, serving on the city council in 1879.

James's son, George Washington Crabtree was in the 1st Iowa Battery of Light Artillery, serving in the Civil War for 3 years. He enlisted at "age 18 years, height 5 ft 7 in, fair complexion; gray eyes, brown hair; occupation farmer". [One hundred years later, George's grandson, Walter, was still carrying on the family traditions of community involvement in Polk City. Walter served in WW I, was Secretary of the IOOF Lodge, and was a carpenter who built many homes and businesses in the community during the '20s and '30s. He served as Mayor and was also on the City Council. His wife, Edna, researched the Crabtree family history, and is responsible for much of the interest in Polk City history that was stirred up during the Centennial celebration in 1975.]

Another son of James, James Adney, was born here in 1856. He worked for the North Western Railway Co. for many years, then bought a farm northwest of town. He and his wife joined the Methodist Church in 1885. "Ad" as he was called, was also a member of the IOOF Lodge #300 for a number of years.

Ella May Crabtree

Ella May Crabtree was born May 1, 1865. She was a granddaughter of John Sr. and Mary through their youngest son, George. She operated a dress making shop "on the south side of [the] Polk City Park." Her younger brothers, Frank and Robert stayed with her to attend the town school. She later married and moved gradually west, spending her later years in Hollywood, California.

Mary and Henry Crabtree

Mary and Henry Crabtree, were children of John Sr. and Mary who were born in Ohio and came west with them in 1846, the first year of settlement in Polk County. At the age of 22, Mary received the first marriage certificate issued in Polk County. The wedding was Feb. 1, 1848. She was not the first bride in the county, but the county government was by that time finally established well enough to keep track of such things. She became the wife of Cal Burt. Burt had been widowed a year earlier, his wife being the first white settler to die in Madison Township. He was left with a small son, whom Mary mothered.

Henry came with the family to Polk City at the age of thirteen and attended the Polk City School. He served in the Civil War, being severely wounded in the shoulder at Milliken's Bend, Louisiana. He came back to Polk City to farm. He was a charter member of the Masonic Operative Lodge, #308, and he and his wife Daphney were charter members of Samaritan Rebakah [sic] Lodge #89 in October of 1877. They didn't remain in Polk City, but left a diary that gives some insight into the pioneer period. It records their journey by wagon in 1878 from Polk City to Red Willow County, Nebraska. The wagon usually traveled between 22 and 37 miles per day. They "laid over" on Sundays, Daphney using the time to write home, to gather wild grapes, to have a "pleasant day".

You will find no Crabtree in the Polk City phone book today, but you will find Crabtree roots in many family trees.

The Crabtree family was a stable and influential force in the development of Polk City. A family of entrepreneurs, they provided farm goods, wagons, lath and shingles, railroad service, and dresses to the community. They began churches and organizations. They served the community in city government. They contributed mightily to the development of Polk City during its settlement and beyond.

Portions of a dairy kept by Daphney A. Crabtree during overland wagon trip from Polk City, Iowa, to Indianola Nebraska, 1878.

September 14. Left camp at 6:30 am. Traveled 10 miles. Came to a little town by the name of Firth on RR. Wrote card

40

home. Crossed Muasaway creek, traveled 6 miles, tuck dinner seen a sodd house with a lightning rod on it, passed through Wilber a town on the BM RR, also on the Big Blue, crossed Turkey Creek. Went in camp six miles west of Wilber after traveling a distance of 37 miles.

September 15. Left camp 6:30 o'clock, past a catholic graveyard, crossed Turkey Creek, tuck dinner on the hill, cross Turkey Creek the second time, went west 13 miles, arrived at Geneva, County seat of Filmore county, traveled north east 1 ½ miles to Ben Sibbets, went in camp after traveling a distance of 32 miles.

September 16ᵗʰ, 1878. Laid over, wrote home, had a pleasant time.

September 17, 1878. Left camp at 8 o'clock, traveled 8 miles, tuck dinner at Mr. O. H. Harveys, west south west, shot three chickens, crossed a little creek, went in camp in a beautiful little town by the name of Davenport, a railroad station, after traveling a distance of 24 miles.

September 19. Left camp 7 o'clock, crossed little Blue, tuck dinner on the hill, Lue's horse sick, give him tobacco, got well, pasted Nelson County seat Nuckles Co., went to camp one west of Nelson after traveling a distance of 24 miles.

September 20, 1878, Left camp at 10 o'clock, tuck dinner 6 miles west of Red Cloud, dog came to us, pasted through Riverton a lively little town, crossed the Republican River, went camp on Bever creek after traveling a distance of 22 miles.

September 21. Left camp at 7 o'clock, traveled 5 miles, watered horsed got melon and large corn, crossed Republican again pasted through Bloomington, the county set of Franklin county, a beautiful little town, tuck dinner 2 miles west of Blumington, by a little creek, pasted through Nives a little town on a creek, also a mill on the creek, pasted through Republican City, 16 miles west of Blumington, pasted through Alma, the county seet of Harlan, co, went into camp 2 ½ miles west of Alma on a creek after traveling a distance of 36 miles.

September 22, 1878. Sunday, laid over, got plenty of wild grapes, beautiful day.

September 23. Left camp 6:30 o'clock, crossed Rope creek, pasted through Orleans a very nice little town, crossed Republican River, crossed Sappy Creek, tuck dinner 10 miles east of bever City pasted through Bever city, County seet of Furnis County, went in camp 4 miles west of Bever city after traveling a distance of 32 miles, got butter, beautiful evening.

September 24th. Left camp 7. Frank shot jackrabbit, crossed Republican River, tuck dinner at Arappaho 15 miles north of Bever City, met Robert Rhorer, traveled 7 miles east to Roberts and went in to camp after traveling a distance of 32 miles. Robert's well fixt, got a beautiful place, we had a good time, ate supper with Robert.

Van Dorns Were an Important Part of Polk City's Pioneer Era

Reprinted from the *Tri-County Times*, Mar. 28, 1996

According to our Polk City Centennial Poem, there were five Van Dorns in Madison Township in 1847, Uncle Jacob Van Dorn, William, Abner, George and Isaac.

William was born in Ohio in 1824, migrated to Indiana then to Iowa in 1847. In September of 1848, he married Mary Jane Miller. In November (remember, land wasn't for sale until the surveying was finished in the fall of 1848), he bought half of sec. 2, township 80; George Beebe bought the other half. William may have donated the land for the Polk City Cemetery. His 14-month-old son, John, was buried there in November of 1850. John's stone is the earliest original stone at the Cemetery.

Perhaps the oral histories claiming that the Millers donated the land and that the Van Dorns donated the land, come together in this family.

William enlisted at the end of the Civil War in a 100 Days Unit. Benjamin Gue's *History of Iowa: From the Earliest Times to the Beginning of the Twentieth Century* explains what the 100 Days Units were. "During the summer of 1864 when the armies of Grant and Sherman were slowly penetrating the Southern Confederacy and engaging its veteran armies in great battles the Governors...proposed to raise a number of regiments for a short term of service, for the purpose of relieving the experienced troops then on guard and garrison duty in order that they might reinforce our armies in the fighting line." In Iowa, four regiments were raised.

Though a hundred days may seem a minor part to play in a lengthy war, it did allow the fighting men to stay in the fight. His enlistment was a major event in William's life as he contracted a disease in Tennessee from which he never recovered. LaVonne Pierce Whitehouse, of San Bernadino, California, has documents signed by Dr. R. B. Armstrong stating that he "is fully satisfied that the said disease followed said soldier until his death, and was the cause of his death on the 22 June, 1874."

Lt. Hezekiah Van Dorn served in the Civil War. Photo courtesy of Marie Buche

Hezekiah was also in the War. He served as 1st Sergeant in the 10th Iowa Infantry, enlisting in August of 1861. In

'62 he was promoted to 1st Lieutenant and served the duration of the war. He returned to Polk City and worked as a carpenter. Hezekiah and William were probably cousins. Another cousin, William Herbert, also served.

Abner was still living in 1880 when the Union Historical Company printed its *History of Polk County, Iowa*. A biographical sketch in that book says he was born in Pickaway County, Ohio, migrated to Indiana, and was one of the earliest settlers here. He "drove the first stake and helped to lay out the town of Polk City," the Union *History* states. He married Oner Houser in 1857. When she died in 1863, she left him with three small boys, Jacob, Willie, and Isaac.

Isaac was the son of a different William Van Dorn. He also was born in Indiana, and migrated with the whole family. Isaac's second wife, Harriett (Hattie) Northway La Belle Van Dorn was featured in a newspaper article in 1939 headlined: "94 years in this country of ours. Crossed Plains three times in Covered Wagon. Has Lived in Polk City for Sixty-Nine years."

She and her first husband left Illinois for California, March 13, 1860. By April 3rd they were at St. Joe. They crossed the Missouri there and continued through Kansas and Denver. "This being the Civil War period and the soldiers being gone from the forts, the emigrants had been warned repeatedly by the government to cease migration to the west. However…everyone was going to Pike's Peak to mine gold. The Indians took advantage of the absence of the soldiers and would charge the pioneers for damages done to hunting grounds." According to the article, "The Mormons were also a menace…stampeded the company's horses three times during its stay at Salt Lake." In fact Hattie's husband had to pay Brigham Young $80 to get back one of their entirely "worthless" horses. In another story, Hattie was admiring the flowers at Young's "home, which was surrounded by a high wall with locked gates" when she was

44

invited inside. She declined when she found out the gates would be locked behind her.

Hattie returned to Iowa by wagon in '62, and in '64 went by covered wagon to Oregon. Her first husband died there, and she took the train back to Polk City, where she stayed. In 1872 she married Isaac Van Dorn. They both had children from previous marriages and eventually had seven children together. Hattie bought her house on the corner of 2nd and Wood with laundry money. Isaac died May 17, 1917. Their two youngest children, Isaac and Bonna, lived in Polk City their whole lives. Isaac's shoe repair shop at his mother's house is still remembered by some of our citizens.

Mrs. Van Dorn lived to be 97, and was often interviewed during her latter years. In 1940 she had her picture in the *Des Moines Register*, picking corn in her garden; a tiny woman wearing a calico dress and bonnet.

The Van Dorns were an important part of our pioneer era. They will be found in many a family tree with roots in Polk City. I apologize that their fondness of the names William, Isaac, Jacob, and Hezekiah makes it difficult to write with more confidence about how the generations fit together. These Dutch pioneers were sturdy stock, and contributed much to our history.

The Harvey Homestead at Polk City

Reprinted from the *Tri-County Times*, March 16, 1989

Lee Harvey, 301 Summer St., Polk City, certainly comes from pioneer stock. His great-grandfather, Longstreet Harvey, was born in New Jersey in 1778 and was one of the first settlers in Shelby County, Indiana, in 1822.

Lee's grandfather, Stephen Harvey, came from Indiana to Polk City in a covered wagon in 1847, squatters in Polk County before the land was officially for sale. With him were his wife

The Harvey Homestead, est. 1847, featured a full two story log house.
Photo courtesy of Lee Harvey.

and twelve children, his brothers, Lysander, John Gilbert, and Cornelius. "They nearly bought the land where the State capital building is," according to the family history, "but it was too heavily wooded and they wanted more land to farm," so they pushed up the Des Moines River and settled east of Big Creek.

The area around Polk City was covered with burr oak, walnut, and hickory. The land was cleared by hand, field and yard alike. Giant trees were cut for building and fences and firewood, or just cleared and burnt so a crop could be planted. On the prairie there was nothing to build, heat, or cook with. There was no water. The pioneers settled in the thin timber belt of the creeks and rivers, then cleared the timber.

Lee's father, Frank, was born in the log cabin on the Harvey homestead in 1855. "But it was hardly a cabin," Lee says. "They had a large family, so he built a full two-story house."

The cabin was built of walnut logs with a burr oak foundation. Burr oak was the sturdiest wood and didn't decay as quickly, so it was used for the bottom two or three layers. The "cabin" had walnut shingles, and eventually was covered with walnut siding. The inside walls were covered with walnut tongue-and-groove. When Frank Harvey turned 100 years old, a news article pictured him in the doorway of the log house, which was then being used as a coal shed. Frank Harvey recalled in that article that "all his clothes were made at home from woolens woven at a Des Moines mill from wool grown on the farm. His shoes, too, were home made. We took our grain to Oskaloosa by team and wagon to have it ground into flour." Harvey farmed with oxen in those early years.

Lee Harvey was born in the "Big House" on the farmstead in 1904. He well remembers many trips to town, coming "north" up old 415 and down the hill into the Big Creek Valley. He walked that two miles every day for school and often drove the horses and farm wagon over that route to get corn ground at Harmon's Mill on Booth Street. He remembers driving by the narrow gauge railroad, past the place his father said the "old" mill was, through the old Beebe place.

Lee Harvey, grandson of pioneer settler Stephen Harvey, was an important resource for the preservation of Polk City stories. Photo by Roxana Currie.

On Saturday nights the family came to town and his father played pool in the combination barber shop/pool hall under the IOOF building (2nd & Broadway). "Of course we couldn't go in," Lee says. "We just looked in the windows." A boardwalk ran along Second Street from the train depot. On the corner of 3rd & Broadway, was a hotel with a livery stable nearby.

Lee tries to communicate his father's descriptions of the area; "folks today can't understand how different the land was." It was covered with either prairie or trees. There were lakes and ponds and sloughs, so when it rained, most of the water stayed where it was and soaked into the ground. Erosion wasn't a problem. Big Creek was narrow and deep. Some places you could jump across it.

As he talks, a listener wishes to get inside his head, seeing the timber, the creek, the roads, the houses, the people—men and women living out their lives in an ordinary way, all of them unaware they were making history in the process.

Author's note: Lee was a wonderful resource, not to mention friend to me when I was researching Polk City history. I really miss him.

Highway 415 Follows an Old Indian Trail
Reprinted from the *Tri-County Times*, Sept. 26, 1991

All of the surveying, bulldozing and grading going on around Highway 415 this fall (Sept. 26, 1991) made me think of Lee Harvey's picture of the big elm tree in the road in front of his old home place. The home place is across the road from the entrance to Prairie Flower Campground. The photo was taken because the state was about to pave the road (around 1919) and the tree had to go. The notation on the back of the picture says the circumference of the tree was twenty-four feet, eight inches.

Lee's father told him that Highway 415 pretty much followed the old Indian trail up the river—there were no bridges across the river, of course. Probably those trails had as much to do with where people settled as a lot of other factors, for the prairies were not easy to travel on. It was neither as flat as most people believe, nor as dry. Prairies were muddy in the spring and the grasses hid many sloughs all year long. The Indian trails followed the high ground, avoided the sloughs and were relatively hard packed from many years of use.

According to the Union Historical Company's *History of Polk County, Iowa,* in November of 1847 the Commissioners were picked to lay out the first internal road in Polk County from Ft. Des Moines to Elk Rapids in Boone County. "Ordered that Conrad Stutzman, John McLane and Andrew Groseclose be appointed Commissioners to locate and establish a county road, beginning at the ford of the Des Moines River, near the house of Wm. H. Meacham, thence on the nearest and best route to the house of John Saylor, thence to the house of Conrad Stutzman, thence to the house of George Beebe, thence to the house of Andrew Groseclose...till it reaches the county line."

A quick glance at those names reveals that the road was intended to connect the mills in operation in the county at the time. The book continues, "This road was about 20 miles in length and was in a very direct line to Polk City. The road, with some important changes, is still kept up, and is, without a doubt, one of the most important highways in the county." (1880)

Lee's photo of what looks a lot like a dirt road taken after the turn of the century makes one wonder exactly what these early commissioners did, and what important changes had been made by 1880!

The road has served us well. If we still drove horses or drove a few miles an hour, trees in the road wouldn't bother us. If

Who knows how long travelers jogged around this huge elm tree before Lee Harvey's dad was hired by the state to remove it from the middle of the road in 1919? Looking at this photo, one wonders what the county commissioners did to improve it in 1880! Photo courtesy of Lee Harvey.

we could stand to take all day to get to Des Moines, the road would still serve us well. (Even if we could obey the 45-mph speed limit it would serve. The road is only dangerous because we drive faster than that on sharp curves.)

It's interesting to watch a beautiful stand of oak trees destroyed and remember this huge elm tree that people were willing to drive around for seventy years, (right lane going north, left lane going south). What a price we're willing to pay for our fast paced lives.

But times have changed and there's no denying it. There is a positive change to be seen in the straightening of Highway

50

415, too. The new construction carried with it mandatory land reclamation. Before anything else could be done to 415, the tree loss, the grassland loss and the wetland loss had to be calculated and the total project had to include replanting of those natural areas acre for acre.

Consequently, the project includes planting 158 acres of woodland at 22 sites, 63 acres of grasslands, and recreating 14 acres of wetland.

The days are definitely gone when we can value a tree in the middle of the road. But it's reassuring to know the days are also gone when we don't value a tree at all.

Eli Mosier
Reprinted from the *Tri-County Times,* 1998

In 1880 Eli Mosier was included in Dixon's biographical sketches as a farmer and undertaker in section 13 of Madison Township near Polk City. He was born in Fayette County, Pennsylvania, in 1812, his family being from the Alsace-Lorraine area of Europe. The family pioneered in the central Ohio forests when Eli was five, settling three of the first farms in that area. Eli began an apprenticeship with a cabinetmaker at seventeen years of age. In 1835 and '36 he spent some months at the other end of the lumber industry, the "Michigan pineries." After that adventure he married Maria Swan, from a neighboring pioneer family.

In 1847 he came to Iowa. According to Eli's obituary, "for a fine blooded mare, saddle and bridle he purchased of Judge McKay the claim to 640 acres lying where Drake University, Kingman's fine place and the Burnham property now [1883] are." He cleared ten acres, fenced the property and built a log cabin. Then he returned to Missouri to get his family. When he returned the next spring, a prairie fire had destroyed it all, even every stick of fence. Mosier rebuilt the cabin, which at the time of his death "still stands about two and a half miles out on the Ft. Dodge road, known to all as the Old Mosier Place. Here was the happy home established, right on the divide of the Coon and Des Moines rivers."

There was also planted the first orchard in Polk County. According to Dixon's *History of Polk County, Iowa*, the trees produced bountifully during the '50s but were winter-killed in 1857. Gramma Mosier, now 99 and living in Granger, exclaimed when I read to her about the orchard, "Oh, for his furniture. He loved to work with cherry!" She reports that as part of their heritage the family is all "handy with tools."

Eli's wife, Maria, died in 1863 after a ten year battle with tuberculosis, leaving three children, Cyrus A., Lucy J. (Mrs. Alfred Crum) and Cross Owen. Cyrus became the Superintendent of Schools of Polk County in the 1870s and later was the court stenographer in Des Moines. His brother, Cross, was taken prisoner at Brownsville, Mississippi, during the Civil War, Oct, 9, 1863, near the end of two years of active service. He remained in prison until nearly the end of the war.

Cyrus wrote an extensive biographical sketch of another brother, Oliver Orton Mosier, for Leonard Brown's book about Polk County's Civil War soldiers, *American Patriotism*. Oliver was born in Platte County, Missouri, May 8, 1840, before the family settled here. But at twelve he attended Rev. Nash's school in Des Moines, and at fifteen he began an apprenticeship at Almon Ford's clothing store in Indianola. At 18 he became a salesman for an uncle at New Jefferson in Greene County. There he married Amanda Orr, sister of a Boone County judge.

Oliver enlisted in Company H, 10th Iowa Volunteer Infantry, and was elected second lieutenant and commissioned by Governor Kirkwood. But he resigned his commission and became a private to fill the company roster. His business experience then won him the office of commissary sergeant. He served until January of 1862 when a fever sent him to bed for two weeks. He returned to work too soon and was quickly ill again, dying within a week.

The testimony of his regiment was that "No half-clad, hungry soldier ever came to him and made known his wants without obtaining relief from him, even if he had to cut the *red tape* with which the commissary stores in his possession were 'tied up'." (*American Patriotism*, 201) Therefore he was greatly loved by them all. His brother Cyrus wrote, "Though he died not on the field of battle, his death was as honorable, remaining as he did at his post and the duty assigned him as long as his throbbing fevered brain could guide and his emaciated limbs support him. His name will justly be handed down with the heroic thousands of honored dead who freely sacrificed their lived for the sublime and glorious cause of Universal Liberty."

Eli was able to get $30 an acre when he sold the farm in Des Moines. He moved up the Des Moines River two miles from Polk City. According to family lore they moved here to get a walnut farm; no doubt Eli wanted the trees for his furniture. He built a saw mill and continued his furniture/undertaker business. He was also a storekeeper and ran a ferry across the Des Moines River to Corydon.

Eli married again in Polk County in 1864. His second wife, Clarkey Payne, bore him a family of eight children: Ulysses Grant, 1864, William Sherman, 1865, Oliver Jones, 1867, twins Althema Bell and Schuyler Coltar(?) 1868, Juliett Stoit, 1869, Alvin Chester, 1871, Bessie Simons, 1876, Robert Armstrong, 1878, Ellen Florence, 1878 and Aaron Franklin, 1879. The boys were named after Civil War heroes, including their own brother Oliver, except for the youngster who was named after the town doctor. Clarkey died April 30, 1880.

Eli lived until October of 1883. His funeral was one of the

largest remembered, according to his obituary. He was also taken to the Union Cemetery in his own hearse drawn by his own horses, the last time the fancy carriage was used. He was buried in a Masonic ceremony in one of his own coffins.

William Sherman, known as Sherm, helped his father run the ferry. He stayed in the area, farming across the Des Moines River. He and his wife, Martha Waters, also of pioneer stock, had six sons, Ray, Boyd, Wilbur, Cecil, James and Roland; they lost a baby daughter.

Boyd was very active in the Polk City community. He married Alice Stoner, daughter of Sam and Birdie Stoner, in 1926. In 1971 they left the farm and moved into Granger, where their later lives were spent.

Big Creek Once Powered Several Early Mills
Reprinted from the *Tri-County Times,* Aug. 6, 1992

Some phenomena are so unique to their own period of time that they become nearly a symbol for the era. Water-powered mills are that kind of symbol of the settlement period in Iowa, indispensable to the early settlers, sources of great wealth to a few and dashed dreams to many more, but gone by the wayside never to be needed again within a quarter of a century. One historian said it would be "an exercise in futility to try to identify all the early mill sites—there were far more failures than successes. For the first arrivals the Des Moines was a bit too formidable a stream to dam. Its widely fluctuating flow made short work of several early attempts within the present city limits of Des Moines."

The millers settled instead along the creeks that fed the Des Moines. Parmalee's Mill was constructed on the Middle River just before it entered the Des Moines, and was in operation for 60 years.

Big Creek, Beaver Creek, the Skunk and Boone Rivers, all had their share of mills in the early days. The Boone River was considered the best millstream. "It wasn't too large, and the water ran between steep bluffs which afforded good anchorage for dams." But even the Boone River was often too low for the mills during three months every fall.

Big Creek was also popular for mills. The Union Historical Company's *History of Polk County, Iowa,* says:

> This stream enters the county near its northwest corner and about two and a half miles from the Dallas County line and flows in a southeastern direction and empties into the Des Moines about ten miles from the north boundary of the county. It has small belts of timber leaving its banks at certain points along its upper course, and about five miles above its mouth enters the large belt of Des Moines River timber, and having once lost itself there returns no more into the open prairie. Points of timber extending out from the valley of this stream were favorite locations for the first settlers, one of these early settlements having grown up into the town of Polk City. (262)

In May of 1846 Conrad Stutzman came to the Big Creek settlement and erected a mill. George Hammond also had a mill on Big Creek then. George Beebe's was built the same year. Probably there were many more.

The explosion of mills (one report says there was a try at a mill at almost every mile of the Boone River) can hardly be fathomed without understanding the corresponding explosion in the settlement of central Iowa from 1846 to the Civil War, less than twenty years later. The population of Iowa in 1840 was 43,112, the majority of the settlement along the Mississippi River. The eviction of the Native Americans from Iowa allowed for settlement to begin in Central Iowa after October of 1846. By 1850 Iowa's population was 192,214, and by 1860 the number reached 674,913. Nearly 500,000 pioneers moved into Iowa in ten years. All of them needed lumber to floor and side their log houses, and to replace them with a frame house as soon as they could, all of them needed a place to grind live-stock feed, wheat and corn. The local mill was a true necessity, and the fact that the railroads and steam-powered mills made water-powered ones obsolete very quickly does not steal their moment of glory.

A pair of millstones has survived in the family of John Peterson. The Peterson farm was along the Des Moines River, and the history of the stones is unknown. One formed the hearth of the fireplace in their house, and one was outside the front door and was used to hold a flagpole.

Possibly the stone is from one of those pioneer water-powered mills, maybe one of those unidentified tries that didn't pan

This millstone was found on the John Peterson farm, Section 33, Madison Township, west of Polk City. Photo by Roxana Currie, courtesy Mr. & Mrs. Ralph Brazelton.

out, or maybe the one built by Andrew Groseclose. Groseclose came to Polk County in May of 1846. He settled on a claim in the area of Big Creek State Park. Groseclose was one of the early County Commissioners responsible for laying out roads. Union's *History* says Mr. Groseclose was a very prominent person and during the time of his residence in the county held some very responsible and honorable offices. His mill was one of the best. It did an immense business, and was not only a source of considerable income to the proprietor, but also a matter of great convenience to that whole section of the county.

When the first white settler in Madison Township died in June of 1847, Groseclose donated an acre of land to be used as a public cemetery. (For some reason lost to this generation most of the graves were moved to the Polk City Cemetery before 1880, all except those of the Small family, who reportedly said, "Let the dead lie," and refused to disturb their relatives' bodies.) This is now referred to as the Small Cemetery, and is part of Big Creek State Park. Because of the cemetery, we can accurately pinpoint were Andrew Groseclose lived.

His mill is often assumed to have been there at his farm along Big Creek, but the *History of Polk County, Iowa,* states "that the celebrated grist mill bearing this gentleman's name, was not located near his claim on Big Creek, but about two or three miles further west on the Des Moines." That would put Groseclose's Mill just upstream from the Peterson farm.

But millers generally brought their stones with them from the East and took them when they moved on. Why would he leave them?

The Petersons' stones could have been washed downstream during the flood of 1851. Every industry has its hard times, and the milling industry had one of the worst in the spring of 1851. *The Army Corp of Engineer's Environmental Impact Statement* states that the 1851 flood was the greatest and most destructive

ever to hit central Iowa. Other writings are more colorful. Sanford's *Early Sketches of Polk County, Iowa* says, "on the thir-
teenth of May, emigrants forded the Des Moines River, but on
the twentieth, it was full banks and no crossing without a float
bridge. It rained, and rained again—all day, all night—it rained
the week around for several successive weeks until the whole
land was deluged with water." The *Iowa Star* said: "Neither the
memory of the oldest inhabitant, or the natives, nor any tradi-
tionary [sic] accounts from the Indians furnishes any evidence
of such a flood. The Des Moines is now twenty-two and a half
feet above low water mark. It was a rushing torrent, three miles
wide in many places- houses were carried off—cattle, sheep and
swine swept down stream, rails and fences, ditto: until it seemed
that the spirit of ruin had taken possession of the bottom lands.
Fort Des Moines was partly under water, and East Des Moines
was completely overflowed to the second bank, or at the foot
of Capitol Hill." The Oskaloosa paper boasted "our city is the
only dry one in Central Iowa."

An Iowa Historical Society publication mentions mills at
Corydon and Elk Rapids and says "these and all others went
downstream in the freshet of 1851, which provided most of
the high water marks of all time on the Des Moines." One report says Groseclose moved his entire mill to Boone county in
1851, another says he sold out and went west. A third report
makes Groseclose the founder in 1853 of what later came to be
known as Fisher's Mill, a few miles north of the mouth of the
Boone River. In light of the devastation of the 1851 flood, it
seems reasonable to believe that Groseclose was washed out in
'51, making it possible that the mystery stones were his.

Whatever the source of these particular stones, the water-
powered mills down by the old millstream were a very important part of the Big Creek settlement, of Polk City and the entire state of Iowa. The State Historical Museum in Des Moines

has a wonderful mill exhibit along with an explanation of how they work and their part in our heritage.

Polk City Post Office Changes with the City
Reprinted from the *Tri-County Times,* Jan.5, 1995

The first official records of our postal service are in the name of Montacute. Montecute was on the Des Moines River, and according to Dixon's *Centennial History of Polk County* it had a storehouse and one other building. Proprietor John Houser was the first postmaster, appointed Nov. 5, 1849.

Netti Sanford's *Early Sketches of Polk County, Iowa,* published in 1874, mentions Montacute as a rival of Polk City, saying

> John Houser laid out this village and built a store and post-office. Houser did not have a regular mail contract, but used to bring the mail up from the Fort Des Moines post-office in his pocket, once in two weeks. After a while it became a weekly mail, brought on horseback by a mail carrier, stopping with other letters at Polk City enroute to Fort Dodge.

John A. McFarland and Alfred W. Wasson followed Houser as postmaster at Montacute, serving until 1852. The flood of 1851 is generally believed to have washed away this small town.

The post office was established in Polk City on August 12, 1852. Sylvanus W. Baker was sworn in as postmaster. After him came Daniel Spaulding, Porter Hinman, and John Bennett. Bennett was a very controversial public figure in his time. He served as postmaster from November of 1855 through March of 1862, when he was appointed Surgeon General of the 10th Iowa Infantry, GAR, at the age of 56.

Nicholas R. Kuntz became postmaster after Bennett and

served for 7 1/2 years. He was a Prussian immigrant who had come to Iowa in 1856, farming at Walnut Grove before opening a mercantile in Polk City February 22, 1859. Kuntz's mercantile operated until at least 1880, when he was commemorated in the biographical sketches of the Union Historical Company's *History of Polk County, Iowa* as "among the most enterprising and liberal-spirited of its citizens...We have seen lives more sensational in their nature, but none that have reflected more credit in the community in which they reside, for he has always aided in every public improvement that would benefit his town and county." N. R. Kuntz signed the earliest postal contract still in the possession of the national archives in Washington, D. C. August 14, 1865.

The contract was recorded with the topographer of the postal department, "to determine, with as much accuracy as possible, the relative positions of Post Offices." The town of Polk City was officially recorded by section and quarter section, and in relation to the most prominent river (Des Moines, 1 1/2 "nearly" South) and creek (Big Creek, 80 rods North East). The nearest Post Offices were Saylorville, 9 miles Southeast, and Swede Point, 10 miles northwest. On the Fort Dodge route, the nearest offices were at Lincoln, on the west side of the Des Moines River, 2 1/2 miles "nearly west" and Cambridge, 12 miles north east.

Warren Pickard, George Baker, Charles Clark, and Robert Clingan followed Kuntz. During Clingan's appointment, on June 14, 1883, the name of the Post Office was officially changed to Polk, although the topographer's office still records the "Local Name" as Polk City. A postcard or envelope with the postmark "Polk" would be a nice memorabilia from this era. Clingan was murdered while in office and succeeded by Thomas Dyer, then Daniel W. Ingersoll and Conrad Hug.

In 1889, George W. McClean filed a new contract with the

federal government. The area was much more established by this time. The nearest neighbors were now Crocker, Sheldahl and Ridgedale. And a new question on the form places the building 1000 feet from the Polk City Station of the C & NW Railroad, on the east side of the railroad. McClean operated a grocery store. Christopher Schroeder, George McClean (a second time), Albert Gorman, Cyrus Snow, and George Naab ran the office up to the roaring '20s. Gorman and Snow ran a hardware store. Snow filed for a change of site October 23, 1915, 1080 ft. from the railroad, on the west side of the tracks.

Naab, also a hardware store owner, may have instigated a name change in a contract signed November 3, 1924. For whatever reason, December 1, 1924, the name of the office was changed back to Polk City. The nearest neighbors then were Ankeny and Herrold.

April 29, 1925, John Blake became the postmaster, serving a remarkable 30 years while he operated a hardware store. In 1926 he moved the post office to its current location [1995], 20 rods west of the railroad station. Mail was supplied by rail from Polk City Junction.

In 1956, Don Burt began his appointment. The hardware store had moved to the east end of town, but Burt bought the stock and ran a store along with the Post Office until the mid to late '60s. By then the town had grown and the whole building was needed as a Post Office. Burt served until 1981. John Baker served a short term as officer in charge, and in 1982, Lois Burt became the Postmaster.

Steve Syverson was appointed in October of 1985.

A Journey of 1000 Miles Ends in Polk City

Reprinted from the *Tri-County Times,* May 16, 1996

Thomas Murray was the son of Thomas Murray I, who died in 1820 leaving a small estate, not sufficient for the family to pay his bills. After his father's death, young Thomas started on a thirty year pioneering adventure, his mother, brothers, and sisters in tow.

The Nicholson and Murray families "came through together" from North Carolina to Wayne County, Indiana, in the fall of 1825. This was a major journey, crossing the Ohio River into the West.

According to family historian, Kenneth J. Nicholson, it was also significant because on this journey "Thomas Murray made his acquaintance with Miss Sally Nicholson." So began the saga of the Murray family, one that continued until it became part of our history in 1852.

Thomas and Sarah, or "Sally" as she was called were married in Wayne County, November 8, 1827. She was 16; he was 21. Two daughters were born to them before they moved to Fayette County, Indiana, in 1830. Children Larken and Susan were born in Fayette County. The family then returned to Wayne County, where three more children were born before the family moved again, apparently following her parents, John and Mary Nicholson, to Henry County in 1839.

Larken Murray as a young man.
Photo courtesy of Big Creek
Historical Society.

A paper by Kenneth Nicholson contains this report:

Thomas and Sally Murray and three other families, having been urged by previous newcomers to Iowa, left in several covered wagons [10 wagons; about 100 persons] from New Castle, Indiana, in September of 1852, and crossed the Mississippi River at Keokuk, following the old trail through old Fort Des Moines on the east side of the Des Moines River bank, and camped at Thompson's Bend, near Union Park. The next day they crossed the Des Moines River at the Mose Lawson Ford, making the trip in approximately three weeks from Indiana.

Larken and Barbara Catherine Murray immigrated to Iowa in 1852 with a large family group. This photo was taken circa 1900. Photo courtesy of Dick Murray.

Sarah, although unable to write and signing papers with an X, was determined to leave a record of her journeys. Her family wrote things down for her at her request.

Her record tells us the migrating party was John and Mary Nicholson, her parents, Sarah and Thomas with their children, Jane Nicholson Madison and her husband Thomas with their children, and Larken Murray, Sarah's oldest son, with his wife Barbara. Larken and his sister Mary Jane shared wedding anniversaries and in-laws; Mary Jane married Barbara's brother, Erasmus Roof, and they followed to Iowa at a later date.

It is understood they stayed at the Lawson farm several days. After considerable scouting around on each side of the ridge, Thomas established a home on the west side of the ridge, which is the present site of Camp Dodge. Later Thomas bought the Jim Hunt farm and lived there the rest of his life, dying August 3, 1878. Sally Murray passed away in August, 1897.

The Murray farm purchased from Hunt was 1½ miles north of the Lincoln Cemetery in Polk County. It had been settled in 1846 in that first wave of immigration to newly opened Polk County. The Union *History of Polk County*, Iowa, says that Ezekial and Mary Hunt,

> being among the first settlers in the county, can recount many hardships and trials that they necessarily had to endure—hardships that at the present day, would be almost unendurable. They came... when the county, so far as inhabitants were concerned, were very few, and far between. To such as Mr. and Mrs. Hunt, who stood the brunt of pioneer life, and largely helped to develop the resources of the new country, are the rising generations indebted.

Three of Sarah Murray's children married into the Hunt family. Susan Murray Hunt was remembered in the family history by her grandson, Ray Swim, as "the finest Christian woman" he had ever known. Two Murray children married Housers. They also (there were 17 children) married Ottos and Millers. All of these names are familiar ones to Polk City residents today.

Three boys grew up to be soldiers in the Union Army. Two, Thomas and Andrew, lost their lives within a few days of each other in battles in Warren County, Mississippi. An early Murray paper in the files of Dick Skinner says these two young men grew up together and "were real brothers, for where you would find one you would find the other." Both enlisted August 21, 1861, at the ages of 18 and 20 and were mustered into the 10th Iowa Infantry on September 18, 1861. Larken also served in the Union Army.

Thomas Murray was a firm opponent of slavery. His sons were in the siege of New Madrid, the attack on Fort Wright, the Siege of Corinth, Battle of Iuka, and the Siege of Vicksburg. Some of their letters have been preserved in Leonard Brown's book, *American Patriotism.* Patriotic sons of their father they were, for the letters are full of phrases such as, "I came out to fight for my country, and I will fight till I die before I will see this government go down." "You need not be uneasy about us; you know what we are doing—we are in the service of our country."

In May of '63, Thomas wrote, "We had a fight at Champion's Hill, about twenty miles from here. Andrew was wounded in the thigh. It is a tolerably bad wound, but not dangerous. He was behind me. I took him off the field, placed him in an ambulance, then went back, got my gun, and went to work again."

A few days later Lieutenant Hanna wrote, "Yesterday our company was sent out to occupy rifle pits near the enemy's works. All went well till late in the afternoon, when Thomas Murray was hit by a ball from a rebel sharpshooter. Your boys were the very best of soldiers, always ready and willing to do their duty, loved by every member of the company."

June 1st, Larken wrote:

> I suppose you have heard of the death of Thomas and Andrew. I am left alone. Andrew died on the 22nd of May from the effect of wounds received on the 16th. I fear he died from want of care. We were obliged to follow up the Rebels, and the wounded were left almost to help themselves. Thomas was killed on the 31st of May, in the rifle-pits; shot by a rebel from their breastworks. The ball entered the top of his forehead just at the edge of the hair. He lived about five minutes.

Thomas was 22, and Andrew 21.

Nearly thirty when he enlisted, Larken already had five children and one more on the way. He returned from the war and built barns, sometimes with his father, throughout Polk County, and was "well known and prosperous" according to the Nicholson history. His barn-building tools are still in the family.

Larken died at his grandparent's home at 19th and Crocker in Des Moines, July 27, 1920.

Family was important to the Nicholson/Murrays. John and Mary Nicholson came to Iowa with their daughter Sarah, even though they were advanced in age. Mary, in her 70s made the trip in a one-horse cart, and only lived 38 days after their arrival. She was the first person buried in the Lincoln Cemetery in Jefferson Township. Thomas's mother traveled with them until the 1830s. Sarah's brother James Nicholson, known throughout the county as Squire Taylor, was prominent in the early court system. Jane Stahl and Nancy Hunt were Sarah's sisters. All had followed Thomas Murray to Iowa.

Young Thomas had begun his journey West with his recently widowed mother and several siblings. He arrived here with his

Larken Murray and his sons. Front, l to r: John, Larken, Thomas "Lute." Back: Joseph, Alfred Hyatt "Doc", and William Alonzo. Photo courtesy of Dick Murray.

extended family, an entire wagon train, culminating 27 years of westward pioneering. Their journey from the family farm in a Revolutionary War battlefield at the Guilford County Courthouse in North Carolina to the place where he finally put his roots down, Polk City, Iowa, was more than 1000 miles.

Gfellers Came from Switzerland

Comparing two candidates for a teaching position circa 1830 an administrator wrote:

> on the other side, Gfeller is better for methodical teaching, accurateness, and lifefulness in teaching. He wrote a better thesis, is more accurate and exact in singing. Finally, Gfeller has more modesty and more aptitude in learning. So I put Gfeller in first rank.
> The school board agreed, and the highly educated Peter Gfeller began his career as a teacher in Walkringen, Berne, Switzerland.

In October of 1835, the teacher married Anna Marie Moser, daughter of a landowner in the Berne area. By 1853, Peter and Anna Marie were the parents of eleven children, and the school record bears the astounding news, "Our teacher, Peter Gfeller, is going to emigrate." It will be hard to replace him, the administrator continues, especially considering his musical talent, and the fact that a poor farm economy will produce lower wages for his replacement.

The economy may have prompted Gfeller's emigration. Large families were finding it hard to buy enough land to establish their sons in Switzerland. But many left the area because of compulsory military service; the current regime was selling their young men as mercenary armies to other European nations.

Whatever the reason, Gfellers sailed from Switzerland on

the *Roger Stewart* with their eleven children, the youngest being six months old, two maid-servants, and a cook. The emigrants were required to bring along their own food and prepare their own meals on the ship. The cook was a friend from a neighboring school, a young teacher, Peter Lehman. (A few years later, Rev. Peter Lehman married the Gfellers's eldest daughter, Elizabeth.)

Four months after leaving Switzerland, Gfeller was an American landowner, purchasing 148 prime acres west of Chicago, "astride one of the three main plank roads leading to town." After three years they sold their Illinois farm and came to Polk County.

Wilhelm, Christina and P. H. were born three miles north of Polk City. P. H. left extensive writings, now in the possession of Norman Gfeller in the form of newspaper articles from Junction City, Kansas. He described their first home in Iowa:

> which was a log cabin. P. H. remembers when the three youngest children slept in a trundle bed which was pulled out from under the parents' bed at night. The cabin was located near the timber along the Des Moines River and a small creek, [Wolf Creek] which provided a place to swim and fish. The timber yielded wood, nuts, wild cherries and apples.

His memories of Polk City continue, "Sheep-shearing time in the spring was a delightful time for the children. The wool was prepared for the spinning wheel, then taken to a neighbor for weaving into cloth from which clothes were made." He noted that the clothes must have been very well made, for they never wore out before they got to him. "Being near the bottom of the ladder no new clothes were made for me."

A school was near their home. Pupils were graded according to the number of readers they had passed. When he left school, he had finished the Fourth *McGuffy*, and "secretly considered myself among the better educated." The family learned music from their father, and P. H. played the violin, guitar, accordion, and "Jew's-harp" entirely by ear.

After 18 years in Polk City, by 1874 the large family again needed more land. Peter, three sons, and a son-in-law went to Kansas, arriving at the same time as the grasshopper invasion. P. H. recorded:

> when the rest of the family arrived in Junction City by train, March 5, 1875, they found the prairies were bare and black with no grass or vegetation in sight. Millions of grasshoppers had laid eggs, and the settlers were worried about the crops that would be planted in the spring. However, warm weather hatched the eggs before much vegetation had started to grow and many young hoppers died for want of food. Later a [spring] freeze came.

It killed the remaining insects and a fair crop was raised that first year by the homesteaders.

Much of his homesteading experience in Kansas parallels his father's beginnings in Iowa. *The Sunday Union* from Junction City relates:

> P. H. wrote of prairie fires which were always a problem for the settlers. Bluestem grass grew to a great height, and when fanned by a brisk wind, it created a great hazard. Many a settler was burned out of house and home. When smoke was visible in the distance, all settlers began preparing to save themselves or others by starting backfires, and plowing fireguards to try to save their buildings.

He also wrote of making their own fun, often combining it with the work they had to do, like barn raisings and harvesting. Occasionally they had a party or dance. Often they enjoyed just telling stories.

The majority of the clan stayed in Kansas. But Wilhelm had married one of the Alleman girls, Clara. They returned to Polk

County, and the Gfeller name is still recognized and respected in this community. Their story preserves a first hand report of the 1850s pioneer experience here in Polk City.

Log Cabin Captures a Moment in History
Reprinted from the *Mennonite Historical Bulletin,* October 1996

When I first met this rustic relic of the past, I was a wide-eyed romantic about Iowa's log cabin period from 1845 through the Civil War. But early discussions with the experts had convinced me the cabin couldn't be that old, so my heart danced only moderately at my first glimpse.

Oh, but it looked old. It had been reshingled with asphalt and listed terribly to one side despite the best effort of a steel cable to hold it square. Even columbine and blue bells brightening the tall grass around it couldn't create a homey feeling. But it was a real log building, rough, squared logs chinked with some gray, crumbling mortar.

The Neuenschwander/Gfeller Cabin was an early meeting house for Mennonites in northern Polk County. Photo by Roxana Currie.

I made myself obey the owner's order not to enter the cabin, ducked my head through the door and craned my neck to take it all in. The dim interior, crowded with the typical accumulation of rural Iowa's "empty" out buildings, looked less like an old shed. There was a loft over the north end, intact, but without access. The odd windows sitting on the ground in the south wall took on the shape of a fireplace long gone. Yes, it was a house, lived in by sturdy pioneers who traveled here by covered wagon, stumped out a farmstead, and built a community.

The earthy smell of well-ventilated age swept me into the past. I had to answer the mystery of this cabin. What was its particular story? Who built it? And how old was it really?

The current owner was a single woman from Des Moines who had remodeled a pre-Civil War frame house on the acreage into a summer cottage. She had only a tidbit of information about the cabin, but she had faithfully propped and prodded it into staying upright for 60 years based in that tidbit. When she bought the place, the seller had told her the cabin was an historic site. The site of what, no one seemed to know.

The only presenting clues were land records. The acreage had come to her from James Brendel, who farmed it for 20 years. He had purchased it from N. R. Kuntz, a Polk City businessman who speculated in land. Kuntz owned the farm for 50 years, renting it to various tenants. He'd bought it from Peter Gfeller, and in 1856 Gfeller had bought it from the original owner, John B. Neuenschwander.

Applying logic to the land records, the cabin was tentatively dated. Kuntz wouldn't have built it, as he only rented out the land. So it surely was built before 1863. When presented with that information the Iowa Department of Natural Resources was interested in looking at it, and after a look confirmed it was probably a pre-Civil War cabin.

Gfeller was the only name on the land records that any local person still carried. A call to Norman Gfeller, a retired farmer active in our local Kiwanis, added an enthusiastic investigator to the Mystery of the Log Cabin, one who became even more enthusiastic after deducing that his grandfather had been born in it.

Yet, even the birth of a grandfather is hardly an historic event. The mystery appeared to be sealed in the past until a *Des Moines Register* article appeared. A reporter, unable to answer a reader's question about a Mennonite cemetery in the north part of Des Moines, quoted a Historical Society publication, *The Mennonites in Iowa*, and listed the names of the only Mennonites known to settle in Polk County; Leichty, Gehman (Lehman?), Snyder, Gfeller, Nussbaum, and Neuenschwander! (I was phoning the library to get that book even as I finished reading the article.) The meeting place of Polk County's only Mennonite community certainly would be an historic site.

In *Mennonites in Iowa*, Melvin Gingerich writes that John and Peter Neuenschwander and Isaac Nussbaum had been part of a Mennonite community in Putnam County, Ohio, for 20 years after leaving Switzerland. They came to Polk County, Iowa, buying land in 1849, land first being offered for sale in 1848. Peter was 73 years of age. He bought 86 acres of land; his son, John, 280. Nussbaums also bought land in Madison Township in '49. Leichtys came in '50. The Mennonite custom was for visiting preachers to come and lead worship in these small, leaderless congregations as often as possible. When the congregation grew and desired it, leadership was chosen from within the group. In the Polk County group, Joseph Schroeder was not ordained to the office of preacher, or John Neuenschwander to the office of deacon, until August of 1858. That's when the church was officially formed. The cabin had been sold to Gfeller two years earlier, but the fact that John was chosen deacon probably recognizes his leadership of the group over the past 10 years. It seems nearly certain they met in his home, our historic site, from 1849 through 1856.

John had 14 children, and he wanted to provide land for them. By 1864 he had accumulated enough land to give his sons Peter and Daniel each 120 acres, his daughter Anna, who had married Preacher Schroeder, 46 1/2 acres, and daughters Elizabeth and Catherine each 15 acres.

Elizabeth and Catherine were married to John and Jacob Beutler. The Beutlers were the first Mennonite settlers in Mahaska County, Iowa, and it was common for the sparsely populated congregations to go to another community to find husbands and wives for their sons and daughters.

The Gfellers were from Switzerland, and came to Iowa in 1856. Family history records a strong Reformed background, but Gingerich's book lists them as part of the Mennonite Church of Polk County. Peter and Anna Gfeller's daughter, Rosa, married John Neuenschwander's son, Peter. Only the three youngest Gfellers were born in the cabin, Wilhelm (Norman's grandfather), Peter Herman, and Christina.

In writings P. H. Gfeller left for his family, he described "their first home in Iowa, which was a log cabin...The cabin was located near the timber along the Des Moines River and a small creek, which provided a place to swim and fish."

By 1874, the Gfellers also needed more land, and Peter set out for Dickenson County, Kansas, arriving there with the grasshopper invasion. The next spring the entire Gfeller family joined him there. The cabin may have been empty from that time on.

In 1933, Gingerich interviewed 74 year old Jacob Liechty, Jr. He may have been the last to remember the Mennonite Community he was part of as a child. He related that the services were always in homes, and always in German. He attended with his aunt and uncle, Daniel Beery and Elizabeth Nussbaum

Beery, in his overalls like the rest of the men. No one had Sunday clothes, but he didn't remember that anyone dressed differently than the rest of the community.

A partial list of Swiss immigrants in northern Polk County before the Civil War, by genealogist Dave Ringgenberg, notes John, Jacob, and Ulrich Liechty, John Werstberg, Abraham Amstutz, Conrad and Johann Moekley, Frederick Manz and Peter Gfeller. Gingerich adds the Beutlers, Jacob Gehmen, and Preacher Singer, noting that in 1865 Polk City had six subscribers to the church paper, according to the author, a large number for such a small congregation, and a measure of their commitment. In the ten years after the Civil War, at least twenty-five new Swiss families immigrated to Northern Polk County, and in 1879 they organized, not a Mennonite Church, but the Salem Reformed Church.

In 1868 the Neuenschwanders moved to Moniteau County, Missouri. They were part of Polk County's history for only 20 years, yet remarkably they left us a log cabin.

With its history explained, somehow the cabin doesn't look so decrepit. It still lists terribly to the west. It's still very well ventilated. The years have not been kind to it; but it continues to stand, a tribute to the Mennonites who worshipped in it nearly 150 years ago.

Schaals Build a Community
Reprinted from the *Tri-County Times*, "If These Walls Could Talk," Nov. 8, 1990

Daniel Schaal was a carpenter and builder in Germany. He brought his family to America in 1849. They came west in 1856, traveling part of the way by boat on the Ohio River, by rail, and finally by stagecoach.

He and his wife, Christiane, had nine children. The boys were all carpenters like their father, and they often stopped en-

John A. Schaal.
Photo courtesy of
Virginia Schaal

route to ply their trade.

They took a train from Chicago to the village of Dubuque, the furthest western point of the railroad. The last leg of the journey, a three month long stagecoach ride brought them to Polk City in August.

The first-born son, John Adam, known by all as Adam, married Miriam Liechty soon after his arrival. She was the daughter of Swiss immigrants and had journeyed to Iowa in a covered wagon at the age of eight. John and Miriam had 11 children, six boys and five girls. All were born in Polk City; Will is the only one buried here.

John and Miriam set up housekeeping in "the house on the hill" about a mile east of Polk City. It was a log house, but Adam "weather-boarded" it and many thought it was the first frame house in the county. (All quotations are from the Schaal family history.)

Miriam collected wildflowers for her garden: "dog tooth violets, sweet Williams, blue wood violets, yellow prairie violets, Dutchman's breeches, moccasin flowers, etc." Once, someone brought a small cedar from the wood, and this became a landmark along the public road, as cedars were not indigenous to Iowa.

Her daughter, Mary Schaal Rogers, wrote:

Mother was a rare gardener. She acquired this art from her mother back in Ohio, and after she was married, from experience. Her flowers became rare specimens from her knowledge of how to propagate and cultivate them. She always knew where the rare wildflowers grew and when we children were sent to the large wood to bring in the cows for the milking, she always admonished us when finding a new specimen never to pick the flower but to dig it up by the roots for her wildflower garden.

Miriam also managed the farm in her husband's absence. Adam was often away building something. He went where the work was, walking to his current job on a Sunday evening, and staying the week unless it was only a few miles of home.

His skill was very much in demand. His obituary in the Des Moines *Register and Leader*, Nov. 18, 1912, states: "for a third of a century as contractor and carpenter, Mr. Schaal was associated in some way with the erection of almost every building in the northern portion of Polk County."

Adam's own list includes 60 houses, 45 barns, five schools (the two-story walnut building on the square in Polk City and four in Crocker Township), five churches, (two in Polk City) four shops, seven stores and three sheds. He built houses for John and Dafid [sic] and Frank Marts, Henry Sexuar, Peter Sutter, two for R. B. Armstrong, Philip Graber, Dafid Mauch, old McBride, Tom McLean, Stephen Harvey, Ulrich Liechty, N. R. Kurts [sic], Will Schaal, and three houses for himself. The business buildings he built were: a tin shop, shoe shop for Schuetz, harniss [sic] shop for John Fett, store for Kelliston, store for Oddfellows, and two stores for R. B. Armstrong.

While building the school in Polk City in 1863, he may have had a sense of the significance of the building. Mary Schaal Rogers wrote, "My father took his oldest son on the roof where the men were laying shingles and had him drive nails in a group of them, saying to his seven-year-old 'you will never forget this adventure,' and he never has."

The boy, Young Will (John William,) grew up to be a farmer, active in Polk City government and the school board. He also inherited his father and grandfather's skill. He built the bandstand on the public square.

Will married Katie Miranda Grigsby, daughter of a Civil War martyr. They made a home for not only their own flock of seven children, but for Katie's widowed mother until she died at the age of 94.

Will's obituary says:

> Polk City is one of the oldest towns of central Iowa, but when Mr. Schaal was born (1858) it was nothing more nor less than a frontier settlement, governed by the rather primitive rules of society which then prevailed, an inland village where stage coaches stopped and where the needs of the community around it were served. He saw the gradual development of the swampy prairie land into cultivated fields, the coming of the railroads...Iowa had been a state but twelve years when his life began.

Many settlers contributed to the growth and development of Polk City in those early days, but the Schaal's almost literally built Polk City, its farms, churches, and business, from 1856 to the turn of the century. The school building Adam built contributed to that development through the young people it helped educated for more than 30 years. When the new brick school on the hill was built, the old school was destined to continue to play a vital role in the community as the city hall.

We're fortunate to have the old school and bandstand with us, a reminder of the skill, sturdiness and pride of workmanship of our founding fathers.

The Grigsby Family

In her Preface to *Frontierswomen: the Iowa Experience*, for the Iowa Heritage Collection from ISU Press, Glenda Riley dismisses the stereotypical pioneer women. One of those stereotypes was "according to myth, they demonstrated spunk and mettle, became courageous survivors triumphing over even the harshest conditions of frontier living" (ix). Fortunately for us, many of out great grandmothers were strong enough to inspire such stereotypes. I have great respect for the frontierswomen who bore loss with dignity and grace. I respect them for just not crawling out into the tall grasses and giving up the ghost. I believe they demonstrated spunk and mettle. I believe they did become courageous survivors.

So at the risk of being stereotypical, I will say Elinor De Hart Grigsby demonstrated the indestructible spirit that sustained many women of the 19th century. Born in Virginia on Nov. 8, 1805, she married Edward Grigsby April 22, 1825, in Wayne County, Pennsylvania, and set up housekeeping there. The next Valentine's Day John was born, and two years later, George Washington.

Soon after Wash's birth she and Edward traveled to Guernsey County, Ohio. New babes continued to come at regular 2–3 year intervals. She was carrying little William when Edward, only 37 years of age, died on Christmas Day, 1841.

Elinor took six of her eight children to Illinois, near Monmouth. Jemimah (born 6/2/36) didn't go, and 16 year old John may have stayed behind with the Warden family, leaving Wash as the very young "man of the house."

The Warden clan immigrated to Polk City, Iowa, in 1852. John Grigsby and Suzannah Warden had been married and were parents of two daughters by that time. John's brother Cornelius came to Iowa with them and returned to Illinois for his bride two years later.

Cornelius surely found his family eager to move to Iowa with him, for disease had overtaken them in Illinois. That tragedy was common to pioneer women surely made it no easier to bear. Elinor had lost her three youngest sons within nine days during October of 1853. Fifteen year old Edward, her baby William, who was 11, and 20 year old Daniel were all dead.

Doubtless Wash Grigsby was glad to take his mother and sister, Katarine, away from that place of death. Still the man of

George Washington Grigsby was one of nearly 80 men from Madison Township to enlist in the Civil War. Photo (original tin type) courtesy of Bill Schaal.

the house after the move to Iowa, he apparently lived with them until he fell in love with Mary Rutherford after he was 30. His father's early death had shaped his life; as his brothers married and left home he stayed with his mother. Now at last he was ready to start a family of his own.

Wash married 20-year-old Mary in June of 1861. There was a family wedding at Mark & Charlotte Rutherford's, her parents, then the happy couple moved to their own home across the road from his brother John. The next June Katie Miranda was born. The little family should have been safe and secure, surrounded by extended family, extended further by the close-knit Hopkins Grove Church family.

But the shadow of America's darkest hour fell across the threshold of the young family. Before Katie was even two months old, on August 2nd, 1862, her daddy marched off to preserve the Union. He mustered into the 23rd Iowa Infantry, Co B, at Camp Burnside in Des Moines. But Wash's heart remained at home and he kept up a constant correspondence with Mary and their "Sweet Babe."

His letters record his thoughts as he trained in Missouri, fought his way down the Mississippi River and waited at the gates of Vicksburg. They affirm the warm, stabilizing comradeship among the twenty-five Polk City men in the Iowa 23rd.

June 21, 1863, he writes his Dearest Mary:

> I Seen Henry Carr last monday for the first time sins the fight he is geting a long very well you can tell his wife and Grimes I have not heard from him Sins I left him at the hospital but I trust he is well by this time and will soon be back with us a gain for I feel very loanson with out him for we have bin so long togeather that seems almost like a Brother to me. John Boe has bin to See me likewise sins we came here he is in good health and I Seen Burley to day he is well and phips is well and bill murry is well and all the rest of the boys but John Rutherford he is a little under the weather...

Wash's friendships within the company heighten the natural drama of his letters. The closeness that made his war experience bearable at times also made it unbearable. Rumor said Donel Sharp shot himself. This young Scotsman's father farmed just down the road from Wash's family farm. Sharp and his brother had a shoemaking business in better times. What would happen to Emily and the children? George Stevens had been a boy in Sunday School at Hopkins Grove Church, where all the Grigsbys attended, ever since Wash had come to Polk City. He was still a boy, for that matter, when he died. John Filmer was another church friend.... extended family, really. He died at Milliken's bend after sharing a tent with Wash since Camp Burnside.

Wash's last letter was poignant...wishing he could taste Mary's gooseberry pie, telling her not to spoil the Sweet Babe, wanting to be home.

General Grant's report totals the Union losses for the capture of Vicksburg: Port Gibson, 130 killed, 718 wounded, Champion's Hill, 426 killed, 1842 wounded, Big Black River Bridge, 29 killed, 242 wounded, and at Vicksburg itself, 545 dead, 3688 wounded, and over 300 missing. Officially about 9000 Union men were dead, wounded or missing after the smoke cleared.

Many sources put the total for both sides above 20 or even 30 thousand. The Iowa 10th suffered 34 deaths at Champion's Hill alone, with 124 wounded. The 21st and 23rd combined reported 373 men fell at the Big Black River Bridge, and at Milliken's Bend, 50 out of 200 men died. Yet the Union celebrated the Fourth of July in 1863 heady with victory; Vicksburg had finally fallen.

Wash Grigsby was wounded at Vicksburg and died on a hospital ship headed north. His body was buried at Helena, Arkansas, but was later moved who knows where. Mary, Elinor and little Katie Miranda had waited in vain for him to come home. John had cared for Wash's business during the war; the family continued their care for Mary. She was barely 22 when Wash died; Katie Miranda thirteen months. Mary kept several of Wash's letters for the Sweet Babe who would never look into her father's thoughtful gray eyes, or maybe for her own youthful dreams that would never come true.

And life went on. In 1864 Cornelius Grigsby named his newest son after his brother, George Washington. In '67 Mary's father, Mark Rutherford, died. In the '70s the church sent Josiah Hopkins away, after some sort of proceedings serious enough to be referred to as a trial, probably in response to the overwhelming loss of men the congregation and community suffered from the war he had preached for so passionately.

Mary later married a widower twenty years older than herself, Leonard Small. Small's reputation was damaged by an incident having to do with stolen horses. He may have stolen the horses; or he may have been part of some vigilantes who strung up a suspected thief in order to get a confession and accidentally killed him. Whichever the case, he left the area for a year or more. Leonard and Mary Small had one child, Bert, but family tradition says they didn't live together very long.

By 1884 Wash had been dead 21 years. That year Elinor

Grigsby, his mother, died, and Katie Miranda, his daughter, married William Schaal on her 22nd birthday. Mary lived with Will and Katie until her death in 1934 at the age of 93. Her first love, George Washington Grigsby, had been waiting to see his Dearest Mary, for seventy-two years. They must have had a wonderful reunion in that long-sought place where there is neither sorrow nor war, and where parting is no more.

Early Polk City Doctors
Portions of this article are reprinted from the *Tri-County Times*, July 27, 1989

Polk City had several doctors in its early years. The first may have been Dr. John W. Rawls. He came from De Kalb County, Indiana, in 1854, and practiced in the Big Creek settlement only five years before returning there at the outbreak of the Civil War.

The next was Robert Armstrong, the son of Irish immigrants, born in Ohio in January 1828. He came down the Ohio River to St. Louis on a flatboat in 1856. From there he took a sailboat to Keokuk, then came across the prairie on foot and horseback to Des Moines. The next year he came out to Polk City and began his practice.

A Living History Farms report says:

> Dr. Armstrong was repeatedly pulled out of the water of the swollen streams of the county nearly frozen to death, and otherwise endured all of the hardships of the pioneer practitioner who traveled from 20 to 40 miles in making his calls. It took indomitable courage. That a man who went through the hardships of those days was able to live and work till he was almost 80 years of age illustrates the value of a strenuous life in the out of doors air.

Leonard Brown's Centennial Poem says Armstrong "bought out" Henry Matter when he came to Polk City and praised

Armstrong for:

> looking far into the future
> with an eagle eye to business,
> calculating well and wisely,
> drove his stakes here in this village,
> drove them down deep and abiding.

In fact, Armstrong didn't buy out Matter: the two were colleagues for 35 years. But he did drive deep and abiding stakes into the community. Mr. and Mrs. Glen Stanley presently own Dr. Armstrong's property on the corner of Broadway and Summer St. Mrs. Stanley believes he had an office in the house at the beginning of his practice in a room with an arched doorway. The brick office was probably built after the Civil War. *Andreas Illustrated Atlas* has a drawing of the property as it looked in 1875. A fence contains the house and yard, meeting at the walls of the office at the northwest corner of the lot. A hitching post is out front. (P. Buckley Moss has immortalized the drawing in our generation.)

The office seems to have been left empty after Dr. Armstrong's death. The house was the parsonage for the Free Methodist Church for a while. Mrs. Stanley says during the World War II housing shortage the tiny building was home to two women. One lived in the front room and one in the back room. Other than that, the office sat empty or was used for storage and the building was very much in need of repair in 1955 when Mr. & Mrs. Stanley bought it. They wanted to save it because they knew it was very old, but there didn't seem to be community support, so they donated it to Living History Farms in Urbandale.

The office was moved in the fall of 1979. A foundation was built on the main street of Walnut Hill, the 1870s town at the farm. Then the office was carefully taken apart and rebuilt on the new foundation. Moving the building cost $35,000. The restoration was finished, the interior of the building was completed with furniture, medicines and instruments from the 1870s, and the office opened to the public in 1981.

Mid-nineteenth century doctors were generally categorized as Homeopathic, using vegetable based medicines or Allopathic, using mineral based medicines, even poisons, which eventually lead to the licensing of drugs. Surgeons, which included dentists, were categorized as practicing "Heroic Medicine," although they used very little of what we would consider surgery. Rick Wiles has researched medicine for his role as Dr. Armstrong at Living History farms. He says the stomach pump was probably the most used surgical instrument, and purges were a frequent cure. But surgeons had learned a lot about surgery during the war. For example they inadvertently discovered sterilization on the field although they assumed that a wound stitched with horse hair just healed better than one stitched up with silk. Of course the success had nothing to do with the materials—except that the horse hair, since it came from a horse, was boiled before use, and the silk, which came from a spool, was not.

Wiles says most doctors were eclectic, taking what they thought would work for the three fields. But when they put up their shingle, it normally advertised one of these three categories of doctors. Dr Armstrong was also homeopathic, and ran a drug store with Mr. Dyer.

Dr. Matter is listed as homeopathic in *Andreas Illustrated Atlas*. Henry Matter, born in Prussia in 1847, left his homeland to come to Polk City the same year he got his medical degree, 1869. The Union Historical Company's *History of Polk County* says he married Louisa Munzenmaier, a German native, here in 1871. They had two sons and a daughter, Carl, Emma and Victor.

John Skinner was born in Ohio in 1824 and attended Starling Medical College in Columbus for a year before beginning a practice near Keokuk. He received the *ad eundem* degree from the College of Physicians and Surgeons at Keokuk in February of 1855. He was also married in Lee County to Margaret Everhard of Pennsylvania. They lost three children, but the four living children were T. B., Lynn, Charles and Jennie. He came to Polk County in 1857. Skinner was Assistant Surgeon to Dr. Bennett for the 10th Iowa during the Civil War. He was president of the Polk County Medical Society in 1876 and was active in the Iowa State Medical Society. At the time of his death Dr. Skinner gave his medical library to the Polk County Medical Society, which was temporarily housed in the Drake Medical College Library.

Dr. G. F. Hubbard came to Polk City after the war in October of 1865. He was an easterner, educated at Harvard and Dartmouth Colleges. He served the army for a year as an assistant surgeon before his first practice here. During the next decade his reputation grew and he joined the Polk County and State Medical Societies. But in December of 1876 he returned to Harvard for a four-week course of lectures. Returning home at the end of the month he had an accident at the Ashtabula Bridge, "within 24 hours of home" and died.

The Polk City library has board of health records beginning in 1893. At the first meeting Dr. Matter was appointed board of health physician and a notice was sent to the other doctors requesting they notify the mayor of any contagious diseases that "may come under their hands." Dr. Matter was sent to visit L. A. Wienhardt, Mrs. O. L. White, Peter Beckett, and Nevada Ingersoll to determine their state of health. The bill for those house calls was covered by the city, $4.00.

In May the record states, "one new case of measles was discovered at the home of Mr. Henry Riegal, the patient being

Mrs. Riegal and that Dr. Matter had permitted Mr. Riegal to attend to his labors, the rest of the family being quarantined." The quarantine was virtually the only method of containment available.

Dr. Matter was succeeded by Dr. E. S. Day, and then Dr. Armstrong was appointed. In December of 1895 an emergency meeting was held "on account of the contagious disease that is now raging to make some arrangements for better health rules." Mayor Hug presented the rules and regulations recently adopted by the city of Des Moines. They included the posting of a yellow card to notify the public of small pox, scarlet fever or diphtheria, the complete isolations of the patient, the quarantine of family members exposed to any infectious disease, which also included Typhoid, cholera and measles. They were forbidden to "appear on the public streets of this city, or the public highway, or in any public place of this city, until all danger of contagion by spreading of said diseases is past." Travel was severely restricted, fines were set, and methods of disinfecting sick rooms were spelled out. Sealed coffins were mandatory, the body having first been wrapped in cloths saturated with 60 grains of corrosive sublimate to one gallon of water, or a solution of chloride of zinc. Public funerals were even forbidden. The board of health adopted the rules unanimously then voted to notify William Elliott "to keep his boys off the street and also to ask Mrs. Elliot to keep off the streets." A letter was hammered out which was much more polite.

To Wm. Elliot and Family:
You are hereby notified and requested by the Board of Health of Polk City Iowa, to use more caution in regard to letting your family leave your premises on account of being exposed to Diphtheria. The board asks this through kindness and for the benefit of the public health.

Board minutes are very sketchy after that, mainly recording the reappointment of Dr Matter and referring to dangerous buildings that need to be removed.

Then January 2, 1902, another unnamed disease sent the board into action. The Methodist Church was asked to close "protracted meetings for the present on account of infectious diseased." "On the 24th the principal of the school was notified to exclude all pupils from families that have lately had any infectious disease" until they brought a note from the doctor that the family had been released from quarantine.

The last record of the Polk City Board of Health was from April of 1904. Dr. Matter resigned for at least the third time and was again re-elected Health Physician. He, Robert Armstrong and John Skinner had served Polk City through many changes, coming to a pioneer village, ministering to a struggling war town, growing with a booming metropolis. They were ready to turn over the reins to the new young doctor in town, Charles Wesley Tyler.

Polk City Doctor Risked Life to Investigate Religion

Portions of this article appeared in the *Tri-County Times*,
Feb. 18, 1993 and April 15, 1993

D r. John C. Bennett, 1804-1867, is one of the most colorful and interesting men in Polk City's history. A medical doctor and military man, he found himself—by his own choice—involved in one of the most controversial and violent religious conflicts in this country's history.

Dr. John C. Bennett was born in Fair Haven, Mass., on August 3, 1804. He learned the doctor's trade by apprenticing with an uncle and began the practice of medicine in Ohio in 1825. Soon he was well respected by his peers. Bennett was also in demand as a lecturer and was a leader in both the practice and teaching of midwifery and the diseases of women and children during the 1830s. At that early date he was convinced of the need for early surgical treatment of breast cancer in women. Later his apprenticeship background began to conflict with the new educational paradigm taking over the medical profession. A huge controversy developed, pitting the medical school doctors, who often had never seen a patient when they graduated from school, against those who had learned at the side of a country doctor, and had never acquired the education to go with it. Bennett put himself in the middle of the controversy by establishing his own medical schools and granting unauthorized degrees.

In 1834 Bennett moved to Illinois where he married Sarah Ryder. He was soon elected Brigadier General of the Second Division of the militia of the State of Illinois and later appointed its Quartermaster General. His medical career was also advancing. He organized a state medical association in Illinois in 1840.

In September of 1840, at the risk of his successful medical and military careers—and literally his life—he moved to Nauvoo, Illinois, to investigate for himself the Mormon Prophet, Joseph Smith II. In Ohio, Bennett had carefully watched the rise of the Mormon religion, now that new religion was firmly entrenched in Illinois. It controlled enough po-

John C. Bennett, doctor, teacher, military man, risked all to investigate the truth about the fast growing religion of the prophet Joseph Smith II from the inside. This photo showing Bennett as a Mormon militia officer is from *The History of the Saints.*

litical leaders to get permission to form its own militia, separate from the state militia.

According to letters and documented reports in Bennett's book, *The History of the Saints; or An Exposé of Joe Smith and Mormonism,* Smith's route to Nauvoo had begun in 1822 when he found a stone while digging a well. The stone, Smith said, allowed him to "see" things when placed in his hat and looked through. Smith convinced his peers that this new stone gave him much greater powers than even his parents, "money diggers" who supernaturally saw buried treasures and found investors to finance digging them up. When he saw a pair of spectacles in the stone that he claimed allowed him to translate old records, he convinced others that God wished to communicate through him. That was when he became known as "the Prophet."

By the 1830s Smith realized he was limited in New York by his family's reputation. He and his growing religion moved to Kirkland, Ohio, simultaneous to Bennett's early medical practice there. Bennett and Smith may even have been in the same Masonic Lodge in Kirkland. The Latter Day Saints moved from Kirkland to Missouri, where their days were marked by continual conflict, violence, and unbelievable growth.

By September of 1840, when Bennett joined the Mormons at Nauvoo, Smith's followers were estimated at 150,000 and that less than a decade after the religion began.

Ten thousand of these followers populated the "holy city" of Nauvoo, on the east bank of the Mississippi River three years after its incorporation. Another estimated 20,000 followers lived in Hancock County, IL. The two-mile wide Mississippi River created a formidable defense, bordering the city on the north, south and west, and Nauvoo had its own 2,000-man militia.

It was the militancy and military strength of the Mormons

that roused Bennett's suspicion. Through his investigation of the church he was convinced the Mormon leaders "were preparing to execute a daring and colossal scheme of rebellion and usurpation," the conquering of Ohio, Indiana, Illinois, Iowa and Missouri to erect their own "military and religious empire." (*The History of the Saints*)

Bennett's abilities opened wide the doors of the city: Feb. 1, 1841, he was unanimously elected mayor and appointed Justice of the Peace by Gov. Carlin, Feb. 3 he was unanimously elected chancellor of the University of Nauvoo, Feb. 5 he was unanimously elected Major General of the Nauvoo Legion. In May he was appointed Master of Chancery for Hancock County by Justice of the Supreme Court, Stephan A. Douglas.

He was also elected to the First Presidency of the Mormon Church, serving as an elder directly under Joseph Smith. There were only five men in this elite group, men privy to the mind of the prophet. Finally he was able to learn the goals and plans of this group that he mistrusted.

He took each job seriously and served with the same energy and innovation that marked his medical and military career. In his inaugural address as mayor he boldly set out a four part agenda.

1. He would use any means necessary to close the drinking establishments in the city. "I consider it much better to raise revenue," he said, "by an ad valorem tax on the property of sober men...."
2. he would establish a university,
3. he would organize the already existing legion,
4. and he would work towards the construction of a canal and wing dam on the Mississippi to "provide most ample water power for propelling any amount of machinery for mill and manufacturing purposes."

The Keokuk Dam "the world's greatest power plant" is

called the brainchild of the Mayor of Nauvoo, Major John C. Bennett, in State Librarian Johnson Brigham's *Iowa, Its History and Its Foremost Citizens,* published in 1918.

So for 18 months Bennett was a Mormon, serving them with the same vigor he served all else in his life. Then suddenly Smith wrote a note to the church clerk permitting Bennett to withdraw his name from the church records. The May 19th Nauvoo newspaper, *Wasp,* included a "vote of thanks to General John C. Bennett for his great zeal in having good and wholesome laws adopted for the city and for the faithful discharge of his duty while mayor of the same." The farewell note was signed by the new mayor of Nauvoo, Joseph Smith. That was the last kind word Smith ever had for Bennett.

All church records and most public bibliographies say Bennett was excommunicated from the Mormon Church. Nauvoo Restoration Incorporated records call Bennett a "notorious man, who plotted the assassination of the Prophet." *The Revelations of the Prophet, Joseph Smith* (Cook, 1981) says he was "Excommunicated May 25, 1842, for adultery and teaching that illicit intercourse was condoned by Church leaders." (In 1842 Smith still publicly denied both his doctrine of spiritual wives and the practice of polygamy.) The following excerpt from *Joseph Smith II: Pragmatic Prophet,* by Roger Launius and published by the University of Illinois is typical of the Mormon record concerning Bennett:

> Smith also received a letter from…John Cook Bennett, a man whom the Saints had expelled from the church in 1842 on charges ranging from attempted murder of the prophet to fornication. In June 1860 Bennett wrote the young Reorganization leader from Polk City, Iowa, a small town north of Des Moines, where he was raising chickens for the commercial market. He told Smith that he owned many acres of prime land that he would gladly make available for the church's use as a communal gathering center. As they discussed

the possibilities in correspondence, however, Bennett asked that Smith keep their plans secret and that he send him a fictitious name and address so they could communicate in strictest confidence. Smith recalled his reply to Bennett in his memoirs: "I immediately wrote him that any communication addressed to Joseph Smith, Box 60 Hancock County, Illinois, would reach me and be given proper and due consideration," and that he "had but one name and address for the communications of either friend or foe." After this harsh reply Smith never heard from Bennett again. Smith's principles had ensured that he would never associate with someone who did not deal openly. He still adhered to the "rules of Behaviour" that he had prepared in 1845 in which he vowed to have nothing to do with any activity that could not be conducted in the open.

Bennett had left the Mormon Church, whether of his own volition or not. He returned to Massachusetts and very quickly published his own version of the story. *The History of the Saints; or an Exposé of Joe Smith and Mormonism in 1842* opened Joseph Smith's secret religion to the world. It is heavily documented and historically remarkable in that it was written and published in 1842, virtually in the midst of the Mormon explosion.

The book includes this quite public threat against Bennett that was published in the *Wasp*, "Unless he is determined to bring sudden destruction upon himself from the hand of the Almighty, he will be silent." Bennett also reports that just before he left Nauvoo Smith requested to see him on important business, locked the door, put the key in his pocket, drew a pistol and requested a signed affidavit exonerating him of all charges or "I will make catfish bait of you." Bennett promptly signed the paper and left town.

During his time in Massachusetts he originated the Plymouth Rock chicken and wrote a book on breeding and management of domestic fowl. (At least he said he did. Even his agricultural projects tended to controversy.) He toured the east, lecturing about Mormonism and advocating the medicinal value of tomatoes. At the same time he was corresponding with the Strangites, a sect that had broken off the Nauvoo Mormons, apparently considering joining them.

John Cook Bennett came to Polk City in 1854. He practiced medicine in Polk City, Des Moines, and Rising Sun, and was a charter member of the Rising Sun Christian Church. But the Mormon controversy still followed him. Dixon's *Centennial History of Polk County* records an incident in the old stagecoach barns in Des Moines in which "Dr. Bennett was compelled to suppress the sale of his work *The History of the Saints*. Ropes and revolvers were freely used to bring about this result."

But in Polk County, as always, the doctor quickly rose to the top. Bennett was elected president of the Polk County Medical Society in 1855 and 1856, and was the Iowa delegate to the American Medical Association his first term. He continued to be interested in poultry breeding and often was an exhibitor at the Iowa State Fair. In 1858 his 5 year-old daughter, Sarah R., died and was buried in the Polk City Cemetery.

Even though he was 56 years old when the Civil War broke out, he was appointed Surgeon General of the 10th Iowa infantry in 1861. He campaigned hard for the appointment. The letter below is on record at the Gold Star Museum at Camp Dodge.

He served only through the first winter then returned to Polk City in broken health. His wife, Sarah, died in July of 1863, and the doctor died of a stroke in August of 1867.

Who was John C. Bennett, really? Was he a talented and able physician, as remembered in the *History of Medicine in Polk County*? Was he a "Man of Mark: One of the strong men who greatly helped the real progress of the world in his day" as mentioned in the *History of Polk County*? Was he "highly regarded for his splendid talents" by the staff of Willoughby

Polk City, Iowa May 16, 1861

General Bowen:

I was down on the 14th and 15th to see you, and was greatly disappointed in not meeting with you. I hope to be at Des Moines again before you leave.

Please send commissions for the "Polk City Union Guards" for Nathan McCalla, captain, Charles J. Clark, 1st Lieutenant, Josiah Hopkins, 2nd Lieutenant.

You can fill them out and hand them to Lt. Clark who bears this letter.

Please remember me on the new staff after the law is enacted.

Yours Truly
J. C. Bennett

University *(The History of the Saints)*?

Or was he a charlatan who sold medical diplomas, who was dismissed by Willoughby, who deserted his wife and was excommunicated from the church, as Mormon Church history has recorded him?

There is certainly a mystery in the conflicting records, but in Polk County Bennett was a highly respected member of the community, even though consistently referred to as eccentric, especially concerning his poultry breeding and commitment to tomatoes. But then, we probably have worse skeletons in our closet than poultry and tomato breeders.

July 4ᵗʰ Celebration During Civil War
Reprinted from the *Tri-County Times,* June 27, 1996

From pioneer times Iowans have worked hard and often worked alone at their tasks. Because of that, a tradition of getting together to celebrate special occasions became cherished part of our way of life. One of the major social events on the pioneer calendar was the 4th of July. Beginning in 1847, only the second year of settlement, many from the whole county gathered at Saylor's Grove to celebrate the 4th. The only detail recorded about the event was that there was an excellent dinner.

The next year the picnic was held in "a grove not far from George Beebe's cabin." Beebe had staked a claim along Big Creek in 1846, built a mill and founded Polk City. The grove not far from his cabin may be the current town square, which the Beebe family later donated to the community with the stipulation it would always be used as a park.

As the celebration began, Franklin Nagle established the tradition of reading the Declaration of Independence. There was a Marshal of the day, an orator from Des Moines, and a "splendid dinner spread of all that could be got," as recorded in Netti Sanford's *Early Sketches of Polk County, Iowa*. One man was "so patriotic" he walked three miles to dig new potatoes to bring. Another settler brought nothing, and when the table was set it was brought to his attention there was no salt. "No! No! Salt is too scarce at our house!" he replied. Those who well understood scarcity and want didn't question his patriotism, and he was encouraged by his neighbors to eat a hearty meal. Mrs. Beebe and Mrs. Stutzman worked a week to get things ready, according to Mrs. Sanford, who surely did her share of the work, also.

A more exciting celebration occurred in 1863. Copies of

the *Daily State Register* from that time shed light on that 4th of July skirmish at the square. Besides the bloody national conflict we were undergoing, the Republicans and "Copperheads" were both holding conventions in Des Moines during the days surrounding the celebration.

Major J. C. Bennett served as Marshal for the event. Bennett was a colorful local doctor. He had served the Iowa 10th as military surgeon the first year of the war at the age of 57. The Honorable C. C. Nourse from Des Moines, was Orator. The traditional reading of the Declaration of Independence began the program. Mercantile owner N. R. Kuntz, Captain of the Home Guard, paraded his men. A class of Polk City singers performed and a band marched the participants to the grove where the picnic was spread.

The event is recorded in Dixon's *Centennial History of Polk County, Iowa*. Rumors were flying that the picnic would be disturbed by the Anti-Union element and Captain Griffith, the County Sheriff, was present and on the alert. While Judge Nourse was "delivering his oration" a whisper spread through the crowd that "they" were on their way.

Suddenly a long drum roll was heard and Major Bennett jumped onto a bench shouting, "To arms, to arms! They're coming! They're coming!"

Immediately everyone was on their feet! Little Polk City had sent more than 70 men and boys to the war and after two years of fighting many had died and the rest still weren't coming home. Fear and anxiety were ready to explode into action.

Judge Nourse called over the noise of the crowd, "Friends, be seated; I assure you, there is no danger!" He then started singing "You're a Grand Old Flag," urging the Glee Club to help him out. Sheriff Griffith took charge of the Home Guard, disbanding them and sending them to mingle calmly among the "citizenry." All resumed their seats. The passions of war found peaceful expression as "a thousand voices joined with the Glee Club in the chorus of that grand old song."

So says Dixon, but that wasn't quite the end of the story. Dr. Bennett, always ready to pick up a pen for a cause, wrote two fiery but anonymous letters to the *Register* criticizing the sheriff:

> Instead of meeting the Copperheads who had sworn to disturb our celebration by wearing treasonable badges—instead of compelling them to remove the symbols of their treason from their persons—instead of arresting them as he ought to have done for a wanton breach of the peace, our patriotic Sheriff turns around to the law abiding people of this community and says—"don't you touch these Democrats. The man who makes the first assault shall be arrested." The assault had already been made. Copperheads had already appeared in Polk City flaunting their badges defiantly. These are the men whom the Sheriff ought to have arrested for a breach of the peace. Instead of doing this he interposed to protect them from the punishment which their villainies so richly deserved.

Bennett accused the "copperheads" of forming their own military unit and two weeks later wrote another letter to the editor, listing the men elected officers of the unit.

August 6th a letter signed by Dr. Bennett reported rumors that "Capt. Irving and Lieut. Small's company of dragoons offered a reward of $100 on Saturday last for proof of the authors" of the recent articles. Bennett proudly acknowledged his authorship and again openly lambasted the company: "Are such men loyal? So is the Devil. He who is not for the Government is a *Rebel*, a *Traitor*, a *Snake*."

N. R. Kuntz, Captain of the Home Guard, fully endorsed Bennett's letter and his sentiments. He seems to have had the final word when he wrote the next week: "I would simply say that as soon as Captain Irvin is legally constituted the censor of the press for the State of Iowa I will submit my articles to him for approval or condemnation: but until that time, his hatred of Union men and his reward for the names of the newspaper correspondents will be treated with the contempt due to a notorious sympathizer!"

Those were troubled times. The battle waged fiercely, both in the field and on the home front.

Chapter 3: Ye Olde School Master From Ye Olden Days

Leonard Brown Chronicles the Civil War

This article is the new introduction to a 2002 reprint of Brown's book *American Patriotism*, published 2002 by the Press of the Camp Pope Bookshop, sponsored by the Friends of the Polk City Community Library, through a Community Betterment Grant by Prairie Meadows Racetrack & Casino.

Leonard Brown was born on the 4th of July 1837, the great-grandson of a Scotch immigrant who fought in the American Revolution and nephew of a veteran of the war of 1812. Possibly that's the reason his patriotism knew no bounds. He grew up in Syracuse, Indiana, attending school until the age of 13, then took a three-year apprenticeship in the blacksmith trade, reveling in the three months every winter that his master allowed him to return to school. Already the die was cast—education and Americanism were to become Leonard Brown's life.

In 1848 Leonard's mother Margaret Cory Brown, died, and in 1853 his father, Aaron, brought the family to Des Moines to join his brother Jabez, a jeweler in the city. His sisters Abigail (Mrs. B. F. Frederick) and Hannah (Mrs. J. E. Jewett) were in Des Moines, also. The family settled in October in a cabin "where Lincoln school building now is, on Mulberry St." (L. F. Andrews, *Pioneers of Polk County*, 1908) Sixteen year old

Leonard became a "blower and striker," making horseshoes at De Ford's blacksmith shop to pay his board with the squire's family. In the winter he built fires, swept schoolrooms and earned the tuition to attend the Des Moines Academy, taught by Rev. J. A. Nash.

The next spring he got a position as Deputy County Recorder and Treasurer, transcribing deeds. The boy later remembered a pre-war day when a pro-slavery politician was ranting in the courthouse about the con-

Ye Olde Schoolmaster's photo from the frontispiece of his book *Our Own Columbia*.

temptible abolitionists. "We hear a great deal about them," said he, "but when do we ever see one? No man dares to say he is one." Rev. Nash, who happened to be there, casting a ballot for some issue, had become a hero and role model to young Leonard. He turned calmly about, face to face with the speaker, and said, "I am an Abolitionist."

With Nash's education under his belt, Brown taught at various schools around Polk and Story Counties and finally acquired the funds to attend Burlington University for four years. When he returned to Des Moines in 1860, Rev. Nash had established the Forest Home Seminary, which later became the Des Moines University, which eventually became Drake University. Brown taught at the Seminary while continuing his own education.

Leonard Brown married Nannie J. Houston in 1861. She was the daughter of a strict Calvinist and Brown's letters to her, intended to convince her father of the compatibility of their religious views, are included in the third edition of *Poems of the Prairies*. They reveal Brown as a passionately religious man. He believed in the Universalist religion and, politically, in the Populist Party, far removed from the old line Methodist Church and Abe Lincoln's Republicans: Nannie's father had reason to wonder at his influence over his daughter.

Pioneers of Polk County lists a paragraph of Des Moines business and community leaders who were educated by Brown during his career. He taught at the first school in Story County west of the Skunk River, then at Avon, at the Burlington University, at Ives Mark's College in Palestine, and at Elder Nash's academy. Often in the midst of a biographical sketch for some young soldier in his book, *American Patriotism*, Brown would say, I knew him well: he was one of my students. Perhaps his personal involvement with so many young lives cut short motivated him to preserve their memory and their heroism for posterity.

Brown enlisted in one of the hundred days units formed at the close of the war: Company F, Forty-seventh Regiment Iowa Volunteers. Other men of letters fought during the war; why Brown waited so long to enlist is hard to understand. After the war he served as superintendent of the Des Moines Schools. He taught at Polk City from 1870 to 1875, and finished his teaching career as Professor of English and Literature at Humboldt College in 1875.

Along with his teaching he published *Poems of the Prairies* three times, making considerable changes with each edition. He wrote various pamphlets such as *The Promised of the Prophets, Popular Perils, Money*, and a final collection of essays published under the title, *Our Own Columbia That Is To Be*. He was an educator, a scholar and writer. But he was above all an American. The flowery language of his poetry and books was more than the ostentatious style of the times; he simply could not adequately express his love for his country.

To Critics

I am unawed by all that fools may say;
Clearly in Faith's stereoscope I see
My own America, the great and free,
In her munificence proudly repay
With wreath of fame, the Bard whose patriot lay
Defends, in name of God, sweet Liberty.
It matters not how lion-like they bray;
With hope undaunted, still unmoved I stand.
Thou art, my country, worthy of my love;
I look with pride upon my native land,
And bow my knee to none but God above.
My harp is rough – a chip from Plymouth Rock;
Its strings –the fibre of the "Charter Oak."
May, 1866

Nearly as soon as the Civil War was over, he determined to write his most important work, a book commemorating those who gave their lives in the preservation of the Union. The book required extensive interviews with the families and friends of the soldiers and with their commanding officers. His personal bias was boldly declared in the title: *American Patriotism, or Memoirs of "Common Men."* Grant and Lincoln were not the only heroes of the war. The privates earned their place in history along with those of higher rank.

Common Men

We live, indeed, in an historic age;
Bright names illuminate the shining page;
The name of Grant, four years ago, who knew?
Old Time can ne'er efface that name from view;
And Lincoln—in how short a time has fame
Recorded high his ever-glorious name!
Yes, in remotest climes is Lincoln known;
His praise today is heard in every zone.
And he deserves the fame the world bestows;
To him our country her salvation owes.
Lincoln and Grant – in these few words I tell
Their whole career – *they did their duties well.*
Does not the faithful soldier in the "ranks"
As well deserve a grateful people's thanks?
Had Abraham Lincoln died unknown and poor,
Within his father's humble cabin door,
From wounds received in battling savage men,
He would have died at post of duty then,
And in the sight of God appeared as great,
As when he died the saviour of the State.
How many noble men are lost to fame!
How many heroes died without a name!
Had Charles but kept the people's good in view,
Then Cromwell'd have continued ale to brew;
And had the South concluded to obey,
Grant would, no doubt, be bartering hides today.
So, everyday, in busy walks we meet,
In mart, in work-shop, on the crowded street,
Men, who in life an humble part perform,
But who, if called to battle with the storm,
Would meet it boldly, as did old King Lear,
Their arms are strong; their hearts unknown to fear;

They know their worth, their modesty's as great.
They are the nation's strength—they are the State!
A nation's fame is theirs; their voice, their nod,
The great world heeds – the fiat of a god!

Brown's tribute to these common men was dedicated to his only brother, Harvey, who served in Co. D, 2d Iowa Infantry, and was wounded at Corinth. Redhead and Wellslager, 41 Court Avenue, Des Moines published *American Patriotism* in 1869, less than 5 years after the end of the war. Although its immediacy makes it a most remarkable piece of history, that did not insure the book's success. Maybe common and uncommon men alike wanted only to put the war behind them in 1869.

In the third edition of *Poems of the Prairies* Brown includes "Reminiscences," including these dairy entries:

...the time and money spent in writing it [*American Patriotism*] will increase the cost to two dollars per copy. I sell the edition for $3.50 per copy. I cannot tell what will be the end of this enterprise— whether successful or not. Mr. Allen seemed to lose confidence in the success of the undertaking and required from me a mortgage on our home which we gave.

September 1, 1869
I have not yet sold enough copies of my book in memory of deceased soldiers to pay the debt, and don't believe that I shall be able to. It is acknowledged to be all that could have been desired, as a monumental offering; but people are not so ready to contribute to have soldiers, who died for their country, remembered, as we might think. I expect that we shall not be able to save our homestead...

August 1, 1872
We live still in Polk County— have purchased a home in the country— a beautiful place fifteen miles north of Des Moines, near the Des Moines River, and three-fourths of a mile south of Polk City. Our house is built on "Hunter's Ridge" — four acres of beautiful

grove and hill and three of a rich and beautiful garden spot. We are doing well enough...

American Patriotism then can hardly be considered a successful book. It was far from a best seller. The publisher decided not to back it and Brown lost his home by publishing it. Yet from our perspective more than a hundred years later, it is truly "all that could have been desired, as a monumental offering." It contains biographical sketches of every Polk County soldier who died during the Civil War. Most entries include letters and personal information that could only be obtained so shortly after the war. Captain Walker, himself a Polk County livestock breeder, gave Brown comments about nearly every man he commanded.

American Patriotism is a unique and comprehensive look at Polk County's contribution to the Civil War. But it is also a remarkable opportunity to peer into the very thought of America thought during the time period of the war. Mark A. Noll in *A History of Christianity in America and Canada* (Eerdmans Publishing Co., Grand Rapids, Michigan, 1992, 243) writes: "The line between religion and politics has always been a thin one in America. In the heyday of 'Evangelical America,' [1800-1865] it was virtually non-existent." The soldier's letters record a nearly universal devotion to a God/Country ideal that seems contrived to us in Post-Christian America. Joseph Mills of Company G, 10th Iowa, wrote before he died, "I feel as though I could face the enemy with cheerfulness and without fear, knowing that if I should fall while in the act of discharging my duty, I would be serving God and my country. I could not die in a better cause" (*American Patriotism*, 197). Genealogists with Southern ancestors confirm that Confederate soldiers' letters embrace the same God/Country unit. A remarkable example of this kind on thinking existed here in Madison Township at Hopkins Grove.

Josiah Hopkins, patriarch of both the church and community at Hopkins Grove was a staunch abolitionist known to shelter escaping slaves. He was as active as anyone in the community in raising a regiment. He himself had enlisted as chaplain in the 10th Iowa in August of 1861, but due to his age served only 10 months. Again at the end of the war he joined a hundred days unit as a major. Because of Hopkins's influence as a church leader, George Washington Grigsby and the other soldiers from Hopkins Grove enlisted to fight slavery as a moral issue and the war as a religious duty. Grigsby's disillusionment was evident when he wrote:

> I tell you it is hard for a man to live in the armey and be a Christian still I will try and do so our chaplin has preached to us wonce sins we left camp burnsides and that onely a haf a hours length it is intirely diferant from what I thought it would I thought we would have preaching nearly every Sunday so when you go to church I want you to remember me in your prayers that I may be gided rite in all things

Grigsby was fighting a religious war, thus his surprise that Christian living and teaching were not given priority in the soldier's daily life. Fellow church member and 10th Iowa soldier, Enoch Beighler, also mentioned in a letter his amazement that the army didn't have regular Sunday church services when he wrote home.

At least twenty men enlisted from the little church at Hopkins Grove. George Crawford Stevens, John Filmore, Wash Grigsby, Caswell Murray, J. R. Shearer, David Grimes, William Johnson, and Enoch Beighler died. The overwhelming corporate loss is thought by some to have caused Hopkins to leave the area in the 1870s, after some sort of proceedings formal enough to be referred to in the Hopkins Grove Church history as a trial.

If the soldiers exemplify the era of American Evangelicalism, Brown's continued writings record the transition. After *American Patriotism* he keeps the rhetoric of evangelism but moves solidly into the post war social gospel. He considers himself a devoted Christian yet boldly expresses disbelief in the divinity of Christ and the literal interpretation of the Bible, basic tenets of pre-Civil War Christianity. Yet the God/Country unit remains central to everything Leonard Brown writes.

His final collection of essays, and in his own mind his most important work, *Our Own Columbia That is To Be,* was published in Des Moines in 1908. In the preface he quotes Plato, "No man can know the right and do the wrong," then continues, "so it would appear that the great end of human effort should be to dispel ignorance, that is to say, to do missionary work." He then lists the "four gigantic evils that society must cease to support: (1) the liquor evil; (2) the nicotine-drug evil; (3) the disorderly house evil: and (4) the divorce court evil. It has been thought that the schoolhouse on the hilltop will rid us of these evils. And I believe it will." Now that America had successfully abolished the evil of slavery, it was destined to abolish evil entirely and to usher in a new era of enlightenment and morality.

So at the end of his life, as at it's beginning, America was Leonard Brown's shining ideal. He considered himself fortunate to live in a time when Americans were given the opportunity to prove devotion to their country; no, not even to country, but to the ideal of America. Thus the Civil War was pivotal in the life of Leonard Brown, as it was in America. Simple, conservative, rural life was buried with the common soldiers. The complex urban age was born. Without the war, Brown would have remained a simple poet and historian—another schoolteacher. He would not have become the familiar (to that era) self-promoter, lecturing from town to town as he did finish his career. Fate had placed his generation at the fulcrum. Hundreds of thousands of Iowans, a thousand of Polk County's common men, had the opportunity to be godly patriots. They were willing, yes happy, to lay down their lives for their God and Country, proving to the ages to come, they were not common men at all.

Chapter 4: Establishing a Community

If These Walls Could Talk, Part 1
Reprinted from the *Tri-County Times,* Nov. 1, 1990

In 1863, John Adam Schaal built a log schoolhouse in Polk City. It was needed so the children of the town would not have to walk out to the country school up north.

The new school was built entirely from black walnut trees cut down near the Corydon Bridge (approximately where Sandpiper Beach is today.) The Des Moines River valley contained the largest concentration of black walnut trees in the world. Walnut was the wood most commonly used in construction in the 1800s.

Seventy-six year old [in 1990] Jerry Parker of Des Moines worked with black walnut all his life and made a study of the wood. He is convinced the building is the largest walnut structure in the world. Without question it is the largest in Iowa.

When the school opened, John de Moss became the first schoolteacher. Many other names common to this area are recorded as school teachers: Desire Matter, Mrs. P. P. Bristow, Catherine Messersmith, Mrs. Nutting, Mr. Mosier and Robert Wilson—are but a few.

The building was also used for church meetings on Sundays. Thompson Bird, founder of the first Presbyterian Church

Still known by many as "the old City Hall," the current
Big Creek Historical Society Museum was originally built as a school.
Photo courtesy of Big Creek Historical Society.

in Des Moines, came out to hold services in the new building. He had been preaching in George Beebe's cabin on Sundays since 1848.

The colorful Kentucky frontiersman, D. C. Marts, preached in the schoolhouse. He had staked his claim near Big Creek in 1846 and brought his family here the next year. He had a chair factory, his lathe turning out hickory chairs with bark seats and back. The factory was swept away in the big flood of 1851, when water was up to the foot of what's now Capital Hill.

Marts then opened a tavern in the busy Big Creek settlement serving cornbread and bacon for a quarter or chicken fixins for half-dollar. He always dressed in jeans and a frontiersman's jacket, and started services by singing at the top of his lungs.

Leonard Brown was Superintendent of Schools in Des Moines and Polk County after the Civil War. He lost his house in Des Moines in the publishing of a book about the Civil War dead from Polk County, and moved to a farm 1½ miles south of Polk City in 1871, when he became involved with the Polk City school.

He was a celebrated author in his day. His book, *Poems of the Prairies*, was the first book of poetry published in Iowa. The third edition of the book, published in 1879, contained our Centennial Poem, written about the settlement of Polk City, (for the American centennial in 1878) and diary entries including his thoughts on the move to Polk City and descriptions of the beautiful farm on Hunters' Run.

Brown left the area to become a professor of literature and English at Humbolt College in 1875, but soon returned and spent the remainder of his life writing and lecturing on social issues.

For thirty years, Polk City's children attended the old school on the square. The histories of all these children, if we knew them, would be as interesting and varied as the lives of the ones who taught and preached there.

In 1893, the "new school" on the hill was built, and the era of the old school house was over. But the old building was destined be become a permanent place of influence in the town of Polk City, our city hall.

Polk City's Uncertain Railroad Past
Reprinted from the *Tri-County Times*, Nov. 10, 1994

When J. M. Dixon edited the *Centennial History of Polk County* in 1876, he wrote that Madison Township was rich in natural resources. "Everything considered, this township occupies a good position; and Polk City, with its railroad and other advantages, is destined to grow year by year in importance and prosperity." The comings and goings of the railroad were either a dream come true or a nightmare to towns struggling to survive as the pioneer era gave way to a modern Iowa after the Civil War.

An article in the *Daily State Register*, Saturday, August 10, 1867, catches the excitement of the times, if not the desperation. The *Register's* editor, "Ret" Clarkson, was invited to follow the route of the proposed Iowa & Minnesota Narrow Gauge line from Des Moines to Ames. Some Des Moines aldermen were with him, and officials from the railroad. "Full of hope, and with four gray horses and two bay ones, three carriages containing eight persons, a box of cigars and a Ditto of 'Catawba' we were soon ready to whirl..."The carriages left Des Moines at 8 a.m., paid a toll to get out of the city, and stopped to water the horses at the county farm. The party passed several farms, a settlement of "foreigners," and the largest barn in the state according to its owner, Mr. McMichael.

"A few more rolls of the wheels brought us in fair view of Polk City, a place several of us had been anxiously looking for, because Conductor Hansman had told us that was the 'eating station' of the road. It was our first visit to the town, and we were rather surprised to see so many houses, and such a bustling little city." Clarkson writes a glowing description of Polk City. He calls Mr. Bebee's mill one of the best in the county. They visit Bebee's store, along with Kuntz's dry good's store and post office, and a drug store also stocking groceries, run by Dr. Armstrong, "well known to our citizens, and our jolly young friend McKee, also well known in this city [Des Moines]." Clarkson mentions that there were other stores they didn't have time to visit, and concludes Polk City is "the centre [*sic*] of quite an extensive field of trade; and with proper railroad facilities, is ultimately bound to be a place of considerable importance and wealth. The group lunched at the Des Moines River House, and recruited two more carriage loads of tourists, "the Polk City delegation, consisting of 'Uncle George' Bebee, N. R. Kuntz, Col. Charley Clark, William Van Dorn, _____Meyers, and Capt.

A boardwalk went from the depot "south" to Broadway where it turned right and continued to the hotel on the corner of Broadway and Fourth St.
Photo courtesy of Big Creek Historical Society.

J. M. Walker—all good fellows as we had a fine opportunity to find out before we separated from them. "

The group journeyed through a Norwegian settlement, then on to Swede Point. They had a terrible time crossing the prairie between there and the 18-month-old town of Ames, where they all went without sleep from fighting the mosquitoes.

At 9 a.m. the following day, a railroad meeting drafted several resolutions. Resolution #2 was "That the completion of the Iowa & Minnesota Railway connecting us with Des Moines… is the most important work that can engage the attention of all residents of Polk and Story Counties, and that the citizens of Ames and Polk City will join hands with Des Moines in the most energetic measure to complete this connection before the coming winter."

The meeting adjourned at 10 a.m. so as to get back home the same day, but the group was coerced to visit the college farm and the state farm. There they were able to see subcontractors working on the first 5 miles of the northern end of the railway, and "so as to have something to tell their children, all took hold of shovels and scratched and scooped gravel of the Iowa & Minnesota Railway." Four miles north of Polk City, another crew was working under Mr. Mullane, who was responsible for the five miles of rail next to Polk City.

From Des Moines the rail was to be 33 miles long: from Polk City to Ames, 18 miles. "With the exception of one or two slight curves, the line is a regular bee-trail. Near Polk City the Company has a five acre gravel pit of superior quality, and all the grades in that region will be built entirely of filling from this pit."

"The road must be built!" concludes Mr. Clarkson, and the road was built, but not completed until 1874.

Union Historical Company's *History of Polk County, Iowa,* published in 1880, tells us the rest of the story:

In 1865 the Chicago & Northwestern railroad was completed to Boone, and in 1867 the Chicago, Rock Island & Pacific road was completed to Des Moines, and these roads soon began to draw largely on the territory before tributary to Polk City. In 1874 the Des Moines & Minneapolis (narrow gauge) road was opened from Des Moines to Ames, passing through Polk City, and the citizens thereof were measurably consoled and pleased; but one of the most uncertain things is the future of a town located on a railroad. In 1879 the narrow gauge road passed into the control of the Chicago & Northwestern. They at once decided to change the gauge to that of the standard width and to straighten the line, which would leave Polk City nearly two miles from the tracks. This has been done, much to the discomfiture of Polk City, whose citizens are now making efforts through the courts to regain these alleged violated rights.

Polk City did go to court, but was only able to get a spur line from Polk City Junction to town. A bridge was built over Big Creek and "the depot was built nearer to the city on this side of the creek," according to the *Polk City Centennial Book.*

By resolution the city council on Feb. 4, 1894 stated "Whereas C & NW RR Co. has located their depot for Polk City on the West side of their tracks, north of a street designated as 'Bluff,' the street commissioner is instructed to open said street" from 2nd to 3rd street. A boardwalk went from the depot south to Broadway. There it turned right and continued to the Hotel on the corner of 3rd and Broadway.

"Older residents can remember talking the conductor into letting them ride the spur line out to pick up folks coming in from Des Moines or Boone and then ride back to town Free." The trains backed into the city in order to be able to head out frontward after their business was done. But the spur line didn't prove to be a solution. The trestle across Big Creek stood until 1967, but the change in the rail route in 1879 was a step in the wrong direction for Polk City's booming businesses.

Hugs will Always Be Part of Polk City

Reprinted from the *Tri-County Times,* March 23, 1989

It's no accident that Jim and Betty Berggren live on Hug Drive north of Polk City. Hug drive was the way out to the Hug farms, and Mrs. Berggren is a granddaughter of Conrad Hug, an early emigrant to Polk City.

Mr. Hug came from Switzerland in 1872, the only member of his family to venture to the New World. He stayed in Chicago for a short while, and then came to Polk City. There was a group of Swiss immigrants here, especially north of town towards Alleman.

A wagon maker by trade, he found employment in the town and within four years had his own business.

In 1877 Conrad sent to Switzerland for his 18-year-old bride, Catherine Ritter. She also was the lone émigré from her family.

Conrad Hug came from Switzerland in 1872. This photo was taken in the 1920's. Mr. Hug was 83 years old. Photo courtesy of Jim & Betty Berggren.

116

Conrad and Catherine had six children: Elizabeth (Ryan), John, Lena, Gretta (Harmon), Fritz, and Harry.

The Hugs became prominent citizens of the community— Conrad served as a township trustee, a mayor of Polk City, and a County Supervisor. As a county supervisor, his name appears on the county courthouse cornerstone in Des Moines.

He began manufacturing tiles in 1886, later becoming half-owner of the business. The tile factory was on Broadway between Bennett and Booth streets. But by 1910 he had decided to invest in agriculture rather than business. He gradually bought three farms in the area.

Conrad's son, Fritz, was Mrs. Berggren's father. He and his wife, Lulu Sutter, both grew up here and graduated from Polk City High School. They raised their family on one of the Hug farms at the east end of Hug Drive. They were grain farmers and also had stock cattle and pigs. Mr. Hug spent most of his life on the home place, leaving only when the government bought the land in the early 1970s.

There is still some prairie in Big Creek State Park that was part of their farm. Mrs. Berggren remembers putting up wild hay from the prairie "from the time I was able to handle the team." Prairie hay was very high quality, considered to be the best there was, especially for horses. They loaded the hay loose in the loft with the help of a rope and pulley system across the top of the barn. Mrs. Berggren was responsible for the horses on the "other end" of the barn, moving them ahead to raise the hay.

Fritz's youngest brother, Harry, had a blacksmith shop in Polk City. It was located between Broadway and Walnut on Fourth Street. He and his family lived in the big house there in the early '20s .

The brothers, Fritz and Harry, also had a saw mill near the bridge on Hug Drive. Jim Berggren remembers one of the last

117

The tile factory operated from 1880 to 1910.
Photo courtesy of Jim & Betty Berggren.

times that saw mill was used. The men went to "Coney Island" (that's another story) and cut logs, then hauled them to the mill. They sawed enough lumber to build three cattle sheds on the family farms. One of these buildings still stands on the Berggren place on N. W. Sheldahl Dr.

The mill was all in open air. A shack was nearby where the men could thaw out in winter, or eat their lunch. Wood lay all around: cut boards neatly piled, ready to haul away and scrap wood drying in random piles so it would burn good and hot. A big boiler produced the steam that powered the saw, and a coffeepot was always on top of the boiler. The machinery from the saw mill was in recent years given to a museum near Waukee where it has been restored to working condition and is on display.

Mrs. Berggren has several treasures from those early times in Polk City history. She has letters from family in Switzerland, written in German in 1881 and 1884. Berggren also has a wagon Conrad Hug made but didn't assemble, and several pieces of furniture he made. The furniture is beautiful walnut and cherry wood with fine workmanship. It's put together with pegs rather than nails. She has a small wagon, also, the one she and her cousins pulled to town to sell cream.

Mrs. Berggren is the only surviving child of Fritz and Lulu Hug. Her cousins are all in other states. The Hug name is gone from Polk City, but the part the family played in the building of the community will always remain.

The Great Barbed Wire Wars

Reprinted from the *Tri-County Times,* Feb. 15, 1990

Before the 1870s fences could only be built with rail or stone. Railroads were bringing pine lumber into Iowa in an attempt to keep up with demand, but the rapid settlement of land west of the Mississippi was ushering in a new age in agriculture. The large farms and ranches were impossible to fence with the resources available, and very costly to fence with purchased lumber.

According to B. F. Gue's *History of Iowa,* a blacksmith from Scott County built the first wire fence in 1859. It was fairly ineffective for keeping cattle in, but was soon well known throughout the county. A few years later his son devised a barb that he attached to the wire.

The first patent was issued in 1876 to a man from Turkey River, Iowa, according to barbed wire collector Jerry Parker of Des Moines. After that, hundreds of patents were issued and the courts were full of litigation. Even the railroad obtained a patent, a flat barb that was easy to identify. They were losing miles of wire in the western states to thieves.

Barbed wire was in such demand that a trust was organized—known as the Washburn Trust. This tight-knit organization of 40 factories claimed that the results of a suit in Chicago "gave it the exclusive control of the manufacture of barbed wire for the entire country."

Among the requirements of the trust were:

1. Every factory paid royalties to Washburn & Co. for every pound of wire barbed and sold.
2. All plain wire was purchased from Washburn & Co.
3. No wire was sold to farmers but only to approved dealers.
4. Dealers sold their wire at a fixed rate.

The farmers in Iowa held a state convention on April 2, 1881, to form a "Protective Association" for the purpose of "resisting, by all legal means in their power, this extortion." First and foremost in their plan of attack was a free factory in Des Moines, to produce and sell barbed wire at the lowest price possible.

George Baker had been appointed Postmaster of Polk City April 22, 1873. While serving that appointment he invented his own brand of wire and had it patented. He eventually left the Post Office, got some financing and located a factory in Des Moines. Baker and his associates eventually built their plant into the largest manufacturer of barbed wire in the world.

Whether Baker was associated with the Protective Association is unclear from the record. But the Washburn Trust had driven prices up to 7-11 cents a pound. In spite of lawsuits, bribery, and other discouraging methods used against them, the free factories committed themselves to selling wire at 50% less than the syndicate's fixed prices. The Legislature, in a bold move, granted $5000 to the Farmer's Protective Association. Machinery was perfected and the free factories began offering barbed wire for 4 ½ cents a pound. Not only was a powerful trust broken, but the farmers showed the country they were a political force that would not be taken advantage of.

Parker's barbed wire collection has been displayed at the Polk City Flea Market several times, and undoubtedly the story of Baker's barbed wire factory has been told there too. Parker notes that Polk City was better known than Des Moines in those days. George Baker's part in the great barbed wire wars was one of the things that put Polk City on the map.

The Buggy Whip Trials
Reprinted from the *Tri-County Times,* June 8, 1995
From Madison Township court records

The pursuit of Justice is neither easy nor cheap, and the same was true in earlier days. In these buggy whip trials both the crime and the costs may seem insignificant to us today, but the slow but steady turning of the wheels of justice is very familiar.

Be it remembered that on the 27th day of May 1881 that W. J. Schaal filed an information against James Laselle for Secreting Stolen property namely one Buggy whip valued at Two Dollars Supposed to be Stolen by Henry Erwin. Therefore a Search warrant was issued and put in the hands of George Crabtree special Constable. The warrant was duly Served on James Laselle then living in Corydon, Madison Township and the property found in his house, under the bed. The Constable took possession of said property and returned it to Said owner W. J. Schaal. The Said W. J. Schaal paying the cost amounting to one Dollar and twenty cents. —W. H. Van Hyning, J. P.

On June 2nd Schaal filed an information against James Laselle for receiving stolen goods and asked for a warrant for his "Aprihensun." This warrant was given to Constable Crabtree the next day and Laselle was "brought into my [Justice Van Hyning's] presence. I read the information to prisoner. He asked time to procure Council and witnesses, which was granted."

121

That same afternoon, at 2:00, "the parties now being ready" the trial began. J. A Kuntz was attorney for the State of Iowa, prosecuting James Laselle for Larceny and Receiving Stolen Goods. J. M. Walker was counsel for the defendant.

Walker plead "not guilty" for his client. Witnesses for the defendant were Peter Lint, Wm. Cammel, James Mercer, Henry Ervin, Mary Laselle, Joshua Minick, Doe Lint, and Wm. Meekins. Witnesses for the State were George Crabtree, Wm. Meekins, Joshua Minick, and Lena Minick. The witnesses were "sworn and examined" and Van Hyning found the defendant "Not Guilty." He assigned cost of the trial to the State, $23.15.

On June 6th, Henry Erwin was brought to trial for Petit Larceny and again witnesses were called. Witnesses for the State were Charles Weese, Doe Lint, George Crabtree, and Joshua Minick. Witnesses for the Defendant were James Laselle, Mary Laselle, John Crabtree, Samuel Lint, and Doe Lint.

All were sworn in and Mr. Schaal was the first to take the stand. Attorney Kuntz examined his witnesses and rested his case. Attorney Walker examined his witnesses and called for a decision.

Van Hyning seems to be pinched by those wheels of justice as he writes, "And now according to the evidence given on both sides my verdict is not guilty as charged in the information. The prisoner be released and the State pay the cost," $24.05.

Half of the cost of this second trial was the Constable fees: for serving subpoena .75, mileage .60, copy .10 for Constable Schrader. For special Constable George Crabtree: serving subpoena for state .75, mileage .60, serving warrant .50, mileage 1.30, Prisoner's Board, 4.00, watching prisoner 4.00, one day attendance at court 1.00. The actual court costs were 4.50, and the remainder of the amount was paid to the various witnesses in amounts from 60 to 90 cents. The State of Iowa had now spent nearly $50 on the two trials, and Mr. Schaal had spent

$1.20 for a $2.00 buggy whip which, we might remember, had already been recovered from under the defendant's bed.

But justice had not yet been served. On June 25 and 26 the defendants, James Laselle, Mary A Laselle and Henry Erwin, were all brought to court again on a charge of perjury. Kuntz and Walker were again the attorneys. The State's witness was sworn in and gave testimony, yet Attorney Walker called for a dismissal. Court was adjourned until the next day.

June 27, 1881, Attorney Kuntz made a last plea that the former motions of the court be overruled. The defendants' Attorney, J. M. Walker, was not present. Justice Van Hyning handed down his verdict. "The Decision of the court is that the Defendants are guilty as Charged in the Information according to the evidence, and farther ordered that the Said Defendants be admitted to bail in the sum of Two hundred Dollars each to answer to the next term of the District court in this county and that they be committed to the jail of Said county until they give such bail."

Court adjourned.

Doc Tyler: Polk City Will Never Forget Him
Reprinted from the *Tri-County Times*, Feb. 8, 1996

If you ask anyone who grew up in Polk City in the first half of this century, they knew Doc Tyler. They either were delivered by Doc Tyler, or their children were, or both! An article in the *Des Moines Tribune* August 15, 1929, documents the story of the W. W. Adams family, 13 of whom the doctor ushered into the world. Nine of the Adams's twelve children, Bessie, Jennie, Teddy, Howard Taft, William McKinley, and four who were unnamed in the article, were delivered by him, and the three daughters had chosen to come home from Newton, Madrid, and Boone to have their babies.

Dr. Tyler poses with Postmaster John Blake and his wife, Carrie, front of Blake's Hardware store in the early '30s. Photo courtesy of Big Creek Historical Society.

The article, written on the occasion of Doc Tyler's 61st birthday, calls him "the patron saint of Polk County babies" and claims that "in thirty-eight years of practice [he] has ushered into the world more than 2,000 babies" mostly in Polk City and its immediate vicinity. He is "gradually retiring," the article continues, "and is turning over to younger doctors the majority of his confinement cases. Maybe being present for all those births is what forged such an intimate bond between Doc Tyler and his patients, for nearly all who knew him seem to have loved him.

Dr. Charles Wesley Tyler was born in Greenville, Ohio, July 22, 1869. The family moved to Runnells, where the boy grew up. After graduation he attended Drake University. Evelyn Pickerel came to Runnells from Ripley, Ohio, at 16 years of age. She attended East High and Drake University. She taught school until her marriage to Charles November 15, 1890.

The Tylers practiced medicine in Elkhart for 18 months after finishing medical school, then returned to Des Moines for more schooling. They went to McCallsburg, practicing for two more years, then to St Louis for post-graduate work. They came to Polk City in 1896.

Mrs. Tyler was very much a part of his work, often going with him on calls. His obituary states "from the beginning they endeared themselves to the people of the Polk City community." They cared for the sick together; "through mud, rain snow and drifts, they ministered to the needs of the people."

They were also active in the Gospel Missionary Church in Polk City (now the Evangelical Free Church). She was in the Eastern Star chapter, and he was very involved with the Masons, Lodge 308 here in Polk City, Eastern Stars, Des Moines Consistory, Scottish Rite, and the Za Ga Zig Shrine. For over 30 years Doc was a member of the school board. He was a director of the Polk City Savings Bank. He was also a member of the State Medical Association and a former vice president of the Polk County Medical Association, receiving a 50-year membership honor from the state association.

Yet theirs was a real life, no fairy tale existence. Their only sons, Clarence and Delmar, died in childhood. A niece raised from infancy was killed in an automobile accident in 1942.

November 15, 1940, the Tylers celebrated their golden wedding anniversary. The community displayed their affection for the couple on that occasion. From Doc's obituary: "Dr. Tyler was a man who made friends and kept them; one who always tried sincerely to do his part in making the community in which he lived a better place. He was scrupulously honest in all his relations with his fellow men." He practiced medicine in Polk City for 50 years, and died July 6, 1946, nearly 78 years old.

Mrs. Tyler remained in their home in Polk City (next to the bait shop) "where so many pleasant memories dwelt, treasuring the memory of the man she loved and spreading the sunshine of a sweet personality upon those with whom she came in contact." She lived in her home until she was taken to Mercy hospital in September of 1951, dying within a few weeks at the age of 81.

No one in Polk City would accuse the writers of these obituaries of flattery, for the whole community truly regarded them as wonderful people. To quote again from Mrs. Tyler's obituary, "They were the type of community physician and helpmeet who make their way into the hearts and affections of a neighborhood. They both found happiness in service, and in doing so left memories which Polk City people will never forget."

Fire!
Reprinted from the *Tri-County Times,* July 14, 1994

The first record book of Polk City City Council minutes begins with these words: "Minutes of last meeting was Destroyed by Fire in the night of Oct 21, 1891." Several week's minutes were taken up with buying new books, a new seal, finding a meeting room (at C. Schroeder's) and figuring out how much money they had.

But as the smoke cleared, a special meeting was called. Mayor Eggleston "stated that the object of the meeting, December 29, 1891, was to make protection against fire. A motion was unanimously passed "that a committee of two be appointed to secure an eight-man force pump and two tanks of at least 15 gallons each, on trucks." The same committee was instructed to get 150 ft of hoses and two nozzles suitable for the pumps. A committee of one was appointed to construct a building for the pump, etc. belonging to the town. The pump committee was also instructed to get 12 leather buckets, 6 fire hooks and 4 axes. The council members at this historic meeting were Eggleston, Dallem and, Bullington, Schroeder and Kurtz. Harmon and Gilbriath were absent. The meeting was recorded by G. W. McLean.

During the month of February, the town eagerly awaited the arrival of the pumps. February 8, the pumps had been shipped but not received. February 15th, ditto. There was a general election in March, and everyone was so busy campaigning that they forgot to record that the pump arrived. But on March 21st a bill was approved for $11.87, freight for the pump and another from Kerfort Bros. for the Pump, $120.

March 23rd a special meeting was called. There evidently was a problem with the pump. A letter from Kerfort listed four different pumps at four different prices. There was much debate.

April 16, 1892, the Council convened with Mayor Matter presiding. A motion was made for the council to purchase a new fire pump, which arrived. "The trial was made. Owning to the pump not giving entire satisfaction, C. Bullington was instructed to notify Kerfoot [*sic*] Bros. by telephone: to send a man up and have him to bring a larger nozzle. Two days later the Council accepted the pump and had a warrant drawn from the treasurer to pay for it. Polk City had fire protection!

From the minutes of the City Council, Incorporated City of Polk City

If These Walls Could Talk, Part 2

Reprinted from the *Tri-County Times,* Nov. 15, 1990

Although platted in 1850, Polk City was not formally incorporated until 1875. For another 15 years the city government met wherever a place was available or the need happened to be. (They once met at the Big Creek Bridge to discuss replacing it after a spring flood.) Early records show $10 paid for 6 months rent for a meeting room at Schroeder's west of the post office.

In August of 1893, a motion was introduced to receive a petition that the old school house be purchased from the independent school district for a city hall. A special election was called; evidently the proposal was defeated. Another proposal was presented in September, but the April 1894 minutes record rent paid again to Mr. Schroeder, at the rising cost of $2.50 per month.

The idea continued to catch on, however, and on May 7, 1894, councilman Meek was appointed a delegation of one to bid not more than $600 on the old school house. At the next meeting Meek reported he had done just that, and the council moved to bond the town for $800 and percent bonds for the purpose of buying and repairing the 30 year old building. Bice was absent; Burley, Bullington, Egleston, Gemricher, Meek and Mayor Hug all voted "yes." Will Schaal was instructed "to go to Des Moines and have bonds made and try to sell same." It's interesting to note that Schaal was the 7-year-old boy who was allowed up on the roof to nail down a few of the original shingles by his father, Adam Schaal.

Remodeling was begun that summer. W. J. Bice did the plastering and Aaron Liechty did some work. Finally the recorder was "instructed to procure one lamp for city hall and put same in hall" and Polk City had an official seat of government. The erection of an upstairs stage in 1897 established the hall as the local meeting place, and as such, rent needed to be set. Rents were applied to maintenance.

Improvements were made over the years, but the basic structure remained unchanged. A *Madrid Register News* article March 26, 1953, states:

Recently the American Legion considered making it into a modern building, but due to the fact that the old black walnut lumber would be very difficult to use in remodeling, along with other difficulties encountered, they discarded the plan. So today, the old city hall stands. Despite the wintry blasts and blistering heat of many years, it remains firm and strong, a symbol of strength and endurance found in the Iowa Pioneer.

In April of 1966, progress finally caught up with the old building. Bob Marsh did the remodeling for the city. He found the old fire bell still hung in the cupola, the bell that summoned everyone to the square for fires, emergencies, and the annual 4th of July celebrations. The old jail and offices were changed into new paneled offices. The beautiful walnut staircase was removed and the upstairs basically closed. Yet the old building remains structurally the same, enclosed in a vinyl shell, so to speak. And the building still presides over the pubic square, its pioneer spirit intact. The landmark is a visible reminder of Polk City's interesting past and the early role the town played in the development of Polk County and central Iowa.

One night only theatrical groups $4.00
One week theatrical groups $2.00 per night
All political meetings except primaries $2.00 per night
Dancing parties $5.00 per night
(renter is responsible to hire marshal at their own expense)
"The Band Boys" can practice for free.

Chapter 5: The Polk City Cemetery/Prairie

Polk City Cemetery: A Window to the Past

There are few places that appeal equally to lovers of nature, art, and history, but the Polk City Cemetery is such a place. At first glance it appears to be just an old cemetery, and not a very neat and tidy one at that! But if you take time for a leisurely stroll along the sunny hilltop, you'll find a window into the past.

A tumbling down burial vault is the first thing to catch the eye. Many approach it cautiously, as if expecting a body inside! There's not! A burial vault is only used to keep bodies until burial. When this building was built in 1890, grave digging was done by hand. When the ground froze solid in winter the body had to be stored until the ground thawed enough to be dug, so it was placed in the vault, which is nothing mysterious after all, only a glorified root cellar.

Burial vaults are unheard of in rural cemeteries, so you have just found your first clue to the cultural history that can be learned at this place. You notice a second clue: the main part of the cemetery inside the traditional looped driveway is crowded with late 19th century markers. The evidence indicates Polk City was an urban area in the 1890s, a center for trade when a wagon trip to Des Moines took all day, even an overnight stay.

West of the driveway loop are a group of much older grave markers. Notice that Elizabeth Burt died in 1847. She was the first white settler to die in Madison Township. Messersmiths are buried there; they were sutlers to Ft. Dodge when there wasn't a road or a cabin along their supply run. Pioneer burial sites also abound to the south in a quiet, peaceful area uninterrupted even by the rock driveway. Hezekiah Herbert, the singing master, the large Crabtree family, and Samuel Hays, who sold his claim to the founder of Polk City, are buried here. Large rocks marching in line with the tombstones give no clue as to who rests beneath them nor do the sunken hollows laying in rows. Doctor Armstrong's wife and the controversial Dr. Bennett and his family lie here near those who in spite of their untiring efforts perished from small pox, fevers, horse kicks, and even a few gunshot wounds.

Mrs. Armstrong's favorite shawl is carved across her gravestone and a rose lovingly placed on it. A little girl's kitty curls up on the sunny top of her marker. Weeping willows, flowing vines and flowers are intricately carved into white marble. Nineteenth century artists elegantly turned everyday items into visual symbols of love and hope in the pioneer cemetery. Artists come to the cemetery today to sketch and study.

The tree stump marker is an art form unique to the 19th century cemetery. The broken tree motif, symbolizing life cut short, was made in various heights, and was sometimes repeated in a bench or table. The limestone markers were carved into tree shapes at the quarry in Bedford, Indiana, and shipped to various locations around the country to be engraved with names and dates. If the stone was damaged during shipment, the mistake could be turned into the texture of the bark.

Around the turn of the century gravestone medium changed. Power tools allowed the use of harder granite stones. Indeed, the whole concept of a simple burial site changed to a Victorian "grave yard." Burial "plots" were bought and marked out as property by some means, maybe as simple as a concrete curbing or as ornate as a wrought iron fence with gate and settee. Times had changed. The pioneers with their emphasis on simple survival had grown into the civic leaders, farmers, and businessmen of the established state of Iowa. They had the money for large monuments to their accomplishments and the time for afternoon tea parties in their fenced graveyard.

Loren Horton, former Senior Historian of the State Historical Society, has been a voice for cemetery preservation and interpretation throughout Iowa. He sees the local cemetery as the Table of Contents of a community, from which we can learn about the economics, values, ethnicity etc. of the community. "The Polk City Cemetery," Horton elaborated, "is a good example of that. It covers a long time span and has a lot of variety. Though it certainly isn't the largest cemetery in the state, it has all the elements of a historic community cemetery."

Across the western fence lies an Oak Savannah; majestic oak trees, brothers, cousins and children of the mighty oaks that ruled this hilltop when the pioneers came. The Big Creek and Des Moines River tree belt was open and park like, not the brushy, crowded timber that overtook the rich soil after those first woods were cleared. This native savannah is being slowly cleared of undergrowth and burned by volunteers hoping to restore it to its original beauty and encourage new oak propagation.

Here at the highest point of the hillside you can see the variety of Iowa countryside. John Pearson has been cataloging plant species at the Cemetery site for several years for the Department of Natural Resources. The thing that makes the cemetery so interesting from this naturalist's point of view is "the diversity of habitat. There are steep hillsides, gentle slopes, Oak Savannah, a small creek, and a dry prairie; quite a range packed into a small area".

Sitting atop this knoll with an oak tree at your back you can nearly imagine the wide prairie stretching eastward as far as the eye can see. By delightful chance, a limited mowing budget preserved a few acres of virgin prairie here to aid our imagination. When Isaac Van Dorn was buried in 1852 tall grasses surrounded his white marble stone. Now, a few feet from his marker, the context of his pioneer life still thrives thanks to countless hours of clearing and burning managed by Polk City resident Scott Rolfes. He and many, many community volunteers hauled 50 pickup loads of brush from the prairie on the first two workdays in 1988. Their efforts have been richly rewarded in the lush vegetation that now enhances this historic site.

Tiny pussytoes and drabna flourish in the cemetery proper long before the mowers come. Looking for yellow puccoons and prairie violets under last year's tall grasses is something like a treasure hunt, but as the season progresses each succeeding species is taller than the last. Spiderwort welcomes Memorial Day visitors on their traditional pilgrimage.

In June the prickly pear cactus blooms. Viewing this bright, waxy flower is an event Midwesterners are fortunate to experience. Prickly pear is common west of the Missouri River, but it is an endangered species in Iowa, occurring in only a few locations. Naturalist John Pearson emphasizes the uniqueness of the gravelly substratum of this prairie. "The next nearest gravel prairie is in the Northwest Des Moines Lobe clear up by Spirit Lake, the Freda Haffner Kettlehole and Anderson State Preserve, or west to the Watterman Creek Preserve. Those are really the only similar areas," Pearson says, in all of Iowa.

Evening primrose, Canada anemone, wild roses and larkspur fade as the temperature rises, and purple coneflowers herald the beginning of summer. The grasses, like the corn, are past knee high by the fourth of July. The yellow composites, black-eyed

133

Susan, Ox-eye, and gray-headed coneflower, are higher still.

The mid-summer flowers are chest high, racing to keep ahead of the skyward stretching grasses. Deep purple ironweed, gentle flowering spurge, brilliant butterfly milkweed, fragrant bee balm; the summer prairie is a riot of color, texture, and scent.

Finally in mid-September the grasses overtake the flowers. Evenings are cool, children go back to school, and Indian grass begins to wave its golden plumage against the autumn sky. Not to be outdone, the big blue stem reaches even eight or nine feet, shooting out the purple three-toed seed head that earned its name, turkey foot. The prairie towers overhead, and you recall stories you didn't believe; grasses higher than a horse, higher than a Conestoga wagon, grasses people could get lost in.

You have begun to understand your Iowa heritage in a better way. The pioneers have become real people. You have seen their sculpture express their sorrow and hope. You have seen the child-picked flowers that graced their rough tables. You have seen the savannah that provided their log homes and the prairie that provided for them. You have seen the pioneers grow from struggling settlers into prosperous farmers and businessmen. Your Iowa perspective has been sharpened by a leisurely stroll through the Polk City Cemetery.

Old Grave Markers Find New Home
Reprinted from the *Tri-County Times*, Nov. 2, 1989

What would you do with 100-year-old tombstones that couldn't be returned to their original site?

That became the dilemma of the Madison Township Trustees after the spring prairie burn at the Polk City Cemetery, the first in at least a decade, uncovered two garbage dumps full of tin cans, fruit jars, vases and, of all things, grave markers.

Because cemetery records didn't begin until 1880, it wasn't possible to know where the stones belonged, but it didn't seem right to just throw them away.

In May the Iowa State Historical Society sponsored a seminar covering a variety of topics dealing with the history that can be found in Iowa's old cemeteries. One of the workshops featured Living History Farm's cabinetmaker and undertaker, Jack Settle. Settle was promoting interest in building a cemetery near the church in their 1875 town, Walnut Hill.

Walnut Hill's Mt. Hope Cemetery seemed the perfect home for the Polk City Cemetery's displaced stones. At Living History Farms they would be restored to their original beauty and reset with the proper dignity. Arrangements were made for Settle to visit the cemetery and look at the stones.

Jack Settle's trip to Polk City proved to be more exciting than planned. He came from work—in his 1875-style work clothing, accompanied by a similarly attired co-worker. City police on patrol were curious what these men were doing poking around the cemetery with shovels and rods! But the situation was quickly explained and the men were able to resume their search.

They shoved through cans and jars, using rods to check under the garbage for buried stones. Since Walnut Hill exists theoretically in 1875 they were looking for specific things. For example, granite stones were not being used in 1875 because the technology wasn't available for engraving them.

Settle was pleased with what he was able to dig out of the garbage. Many stones were usable and could be cleaned up to look like new. Every footstone will be used at Mt Hope Cemetery. They are basically plain, flat marble and only need to be sanded with a belt sander until they return to gleaming white. Three appropriate headstones were found, one missing its decorative top and two beautifully-shaped and nearly intact.

The challenge of restoring the stones will be given to stone-cutter Darwin Thede. They will be "glued" together, sanded and the details carved back into the stone.

Settle has been learning by doing for this cemetery project. He is a woodworker by trade and doing research into what kind of sign he wanted above his Walnut Hill business, he discovered that most cabinetmakers were also undertakers.

Settle decided he should have a coffin in his shop if he was the undertaker, so he built one. People were interested and curious about the coffin so the woodworker saw an opportunity to add some reality to people's concept of the "good old days." Death was common and real. People often died of diseases such as flu and measles. Settle's searching through old cemeteries has made him believe that 40% of the stones mark the graves of children under eight years of age.

The Mt. Hope cemetery has been a good addition to Living History Farms' early Iowa town. The graveyard lends an authenticity to the town that visitors readily identify with. There are six stones in place now, mostly children's markers. A weeping willow and some flowers have been planted. Additional stones will be collected until there are 16 to 18 "graves." When the weeping willow gets a little bigger, a mourner's bench will be set under it and footpaths added.

It will probably take two years to restore and set the Polk City stones. Then another piece of Iowa history will be passed on to the next generation; not "saved" as in a museum, but used to make the past come alive in a way that is unique to Living History Farms.

Old Vault Should Be Preserved
Reprinted from the *Tri-County Times,* Aug. 30, 1990

The door is broken. Bricks lie randomly where they have fallen. There's a window in the brick front where none was before. Although time has badly wounded it, the burial vault at the historic Polk City Cemetery has limped feebly into it's 100th year.

In 1890 a burial vault was a common site in urban cemeteries. It was useful for storing bodies in the winter when the ground was frozen solid, or in summer when they couldn't be buried immediately. Less often it was used in the heat of summer if a burial was delayed.

The vault is built into the hillside like a root cellar. The front is 5 bricks thick, resulting in a fairly constant temperature in the interior room. It served its purpose well.

Chet Coffeen was the caretaker of the cemetery for nearly 20 years. He well remembers cleaning and fixing the vault so he could store his wheel borrow, curbing boards, and spades in it. The building was filled with sand that had washed down the road when it rained. An old iron door had fallen off the hinges and lay by the vault rusting away. Coffeen had a junk man from Des Moines come to get the old door. He then installed a wooden door with a lock and repainted the iron bars in front of the door. The vault was such a good place for storage that he even put his moped in it during the winter.

He says most of the damage to the brick front has occurred in the last few years. Until then, the round front rose up in two columns like chimneys. A cement sign adorned the front "RECEIVING VAULT 1890." Coffeen painted the sign black with gold letters and the neighboring farmer, Jim Sprague, noticed it for the first time. The township trustees responsible for the cemetery feared the cement sign would fall on someone so they

The holding vault at the Polk City cemetery was allowed to decay and was overgrown with poison ivy. Much of the damage to the building occurred when the cemetery managers removed the sign above the door for fear it would fall on someone. Photos by Roxana Currie.

hired men to take it down. It turned out the sign was so solidly attached it was a real job to get it loose, and in the process the sign it was dropped and broken.

In the spring of 1989 the Polk City Historic Research Group applied through the library for funds from KRNT Project Main Street for repair of the vault. At that time an engineer determined the structure was sound and the front could easily be rebuilt. But the funds were not received and the township trustees felt uncomfortable using tax money to rebuild it since it isn't used anymore. So the vault continues to deteriorate. Rabbits find shelter there and vandals use its dilapidated condition as an excuse to deface it further. Many consider it an eyesore and wish it were gone.

But there are many people who regularly visit the cemetery just to enjoy the history there. Darwin Thede, stone carver and consultant at Living History Farms for 17 years, happened to visit during the Kiwanis Barbecue last year and stopped in town to get a copy of the "Historic Walk." He said in a survey being taken at the time. "The vault is an unusual feature, not often encountered in small or rural burying grounds. It should be preserved and rebuilt if possible."

No pictures of the vault in good condition have ever come to light. We are left to imagine the owl-shaped face solemnly overlooking the cemetery during Polk City's boom years at the turn of the century. Once it was a symbol of the pride and confidence Polk City felt as it looked towards the future.

What does it symbolize today, lying in a heap on its 100th birthday?

(Note: the vault has since been rebuilt by the Big Creek Historical Society.)

Prairie at Polk City

Reprinted from the *Federated Garden Clubs of Iowa Newsletter,*
Fall 1990, Vol. LIII, Number 3

One hundred forty years ago, young John Van Dorn was buried beneath a sea of waving prairie grass on a sandy hillside north of Big Creek. His family was one of the first families to settle in Polk County. The tall grass prairie was the Iowa they knew. Many things have changed here in nearly a century and a half. The Big Creek Settlement became Polk City, and the Van Dorn family plot covers the entire southeastern corner of the cemetery. But some of the prairie still survives near Van Dorn's grave, one of only two high quality virgin prairies remaining in Polk County.

Restoration work began in the prairie in 1988, a cooperative effort between the community, the corps of engineers, and the department of Natural Resources. Clean up days were organized throughout the summer. Sumac and other brush had nearly overrun the native plants. Pickup truck loads of volunteer ash, elm, and cedar were cleared from the site. Boy Scouts, senior citizens, rangers, firemen, and many others from the community cooperated to bring the encroaching woods under control.

In the spring of 1989 the DNR and the Corps of Engineers cooperated on a spring burn. Now the site seemed completely devoid of life, but the prairie's extensive root system was ready to shoot up with renewed vigor. The seeds of many forbs like

The prairie at the Polk City Cemetery contains the most diverse plant population of any prairie in Polk County. Photo by Roxana Currie.

pale purple coneflower were broken open by the fire to germinate for the first time in many years.

The clean-up and burn was very successful, though the battle with the sumac will continue for many years. Yet the protection of the prairie is much more than a physical clearing of brush. In the absence of laws protecting Iowa prairie, education and exposure are the only tools available for keeping the Polk City Cemetery/Prairie from being destroyed, and for encouraging proper care and management of that valuable site.

The general perception of a tallgrass prairie is as a dreary, brown, lonely place. Once you get to know a prairie, though, it is anything but dreary. Even the grasses display an amazing variety of shapes and sizes. But the flowers are the secret life of the prairie—one of the delights of pioneer life that didn't get passed down to our generation. From tiny puccoons and prairie violets in the April to towering cup plants in August, the prairie is a parade of color.

The parade begins early with tiny yellow puccoons, white pussytoes and lavender prairie. Warmer weather brings the evening primrose, Canada Anemone, and wild roses. Spiderwort dots both the cemetery and prairie with purple, and even an uncommon white spiderwort survives there. (It's gone now.) Delicate larkspur sways above the grasses on a slender stalk.

The cemetery soil is dry and gravelly, classified as a mesic, site and contains species suited to that environment. The most unique is the prickly pear cactus. Prickly pear, the only widespread eastern cactus, is endangered in Iowa. Its June blooming time is an event to mark on the calendar. The waxy-looking yellow flowers, bright red in the center, would be a treat even in a common flower. In the only native Iowa cactus it's a breathtaking sight.

As the spring flowers fade the purple coneflowers herald the beginning of summer. They're quickly followed by the yellow composites: black-eyed Susan, ox-eye, gray-headed cone-flowers. Leadplant quickly blooms and fades, leaving a dusty mauve background for the purple and white prairie clovers. The midsummer flowers are chest high, stretching their heads to keep above the quickly growing grasses. Deep purple iron-weed, gentle flowering spurge, fragrant bee-balm; the summer prairie is a riot of colors, textures, and smells.

Chester Coffeen lovingly cared for the Polk City Cemetery for twenty years. He carefully burned the tall grasses every spring. There was no problem with encroaching trees then. The old part of the cemetery was left to the grasses and wild flowers. A farmer came in with a scythe once a year and cut the grass carefully around the 100 year old stones, gathering "prairie hay" for his livestock.

Coffeen recalls bright orange flowers that decorated many of the pioneer's graves throughout the summer. "And I never mowed them off," he insists, "they were too pretty!" The striking orange flower was probably butterfly milkweed, so named because its brightness is so attractive to insects.

Today one butterfly milkweed remains, down in the draw, all but hidden from view by the still threatening sumac. Its fate is the fate of all Iowa prairies. Unprotected by law even though 99.9% has already been destroyed, an entire ecosystem is vanishing plant by plant. Iowa, the tallgrass state for 5000 years before tall corn was introduced here, was originally covered with 30 million acres of prairie. It is the only state whose dominant natural heritage is tallgrass prairie.

Where that heritage remains, it is not a sea of waving grasses. The beauty and intensity of that sight will never be experienced again. Our heritage remains only in a strip of railroad right-of-way, a slough, a steep ridge, or an old settler's cemetery.

In a modern, hostile environment, prairies need continuous care to survive. They need protection from mowers and sprays, protection from trees and brush, protection from thoughtless management. Otherwise, we may be the last generation to see the Iowa Prairie at all.

Mr. Murray

Mr. Murray had to be called out to finish off that stubborn sumac. I happened to be there when he was working and he told me why he liked prairie.

His mother's family had homesteaded in North Dakota and Nebraska when she was a young girl, but the family eventually wound up back in Des Moines. After her 80th birthday, Mr. Murray's mother was able to come up to Saylorville and see some of the restored prairie there. She was as excited as a little girl, he said, as she walked through the prairie naming the flowers she hadn't seen for a lifetime. She often talked about that trip to the prairie as the highlight of her last years. (June 9-89)

How Can a Prairie Be Saved?
Reprinted from *The Bull's Eye,* Nov. 11, 1998

I was fortunate enough to get a government contract to hand harvest prairie this fall [1998]. It's been a beautiful fall. I believe a lot of people who can't tell big blue stem from a milkweed pod would gladly change places with me, for there is no better way to spend a warm fall day than out on a prairie. The sun turns everything a glowing, golden hue and the wind dances gently through the giant grasses. Fiery red little blue stem and various seed heads from the summer's flowers add amazing color and texture to what appears at first glance to be a brown hillside.

This particular day I sit on the huge Graeber stone at the

Polk City Cemetery (the one so big that even hauling it in three pieces, it broke the old wooden bridge at the entrance) moping as I eat my lunch. I would normally try to picture the cornfield across the fence restored to prairie; a project that's been in the works since 1993 and will easily double the acreage of prairie at the site. The thing hardest to imagine about Iowa's tall grass prairie is its vastness in a world where this patch around the edges of a cemetery is the highest quality virgin site in Polk County. Today my imagination refuses even to work.

I have been introduced at prairie events as the woman who saved the Polk City Cemetery Prairie. It's a title I refuse for two reasons. First, the restoration work done in the late '80s was truly a community work. The Boy Scouts, the Lake Country Senior Citizens, the trustees, the firemen and a lot of private citizens worked very hard to clear tons of very ugly volunteer trees and brush from the site. (I wonder if the person who interrupted my work this morning to remind me of his/her dislike for the prairie remembers what it looked like then?) But there's a bigger reason I refuse to be called a saver—because I know the prairie is not saved. My melancholy lunch is the result of three between-the-eyes reminders I've been hit with just this morning.

I arrived eager to dive into collecting Indian grass. There's no better Indian grass anywhere in Iowa than at the cemetery, and it will be the basic filler of our replanting project. People familiar with prairie know the quality and quantity of grass at the cemetery and someone has harvested it over the weekend. It's gone. Their theft has cost me at least three hours of work and has cost our replanting project an estimated 15 gallons of seed, not to mention the most desirable seed for our purposes because it is on site. (This may seem a technicality, but to restore without altering genetic structure, seed closest to home is always best.)

In my present state I cannot see the amazing comeback the prairie at the cemetery has made in just ten years. I can only see how much has been lost. I make myself walk through the area across the road from the burial vault that has had dirt dumped on it for the third time this past summer. As I feared, there are no prairie species left at all in a thousand-square-foot area. Not a trace remains of even the sturdy little wild rose, our state flower, which only recently lined the road with every shade of pink.

A little further south, the track that a tenant farmer began a few years ago down into the cornfield has become a superhighway. We still held onto hope that we could stop the traffic and the vegetation would come back. This fall someone put gravel on it: another 15 by 60 foot strip of virgin prairie that is suddenly, without a thought, just gone. Both of those sites will now slowly turn into weed patches of whatever seed happens to be in the dirt and gravel, and those weeds will be what people notice, saying, "Why don't they just mow that ugly prairie?"

I would love to save the prairie. Would someone tell me, how can a prairie be saved? Those who don't understand it destroy it, without malice to be sure, but destroy it nonetheless. Those who do understand exploit it, convinced by a high priced seed market that seed on public lands is theirs for the taking, or at least first-come, first-served. Yet whether through malice, ignorance, or exploitation, when prairie disappears, it's gone. I've gone to prairie events all over Iowa. I've seen prairies that really did look like weed patches. I've seen sparse vegetation on a dead looking field declared high quality. And in the context of today—less than 1% of the original prairie survives in any form in Iowa—those *are* valuable sites. But I've never seen anything in all of Iowa like the lush variety of the Polk City Cemetery prairie. Someone tell me, please, how can a prairie be saved?

I throw my apple core to the birds and put the rest of my

lunch back in the car. I turn on a tape and roll the car windows down. The only possible way to improve an afternoon on the prairie is with piano accompaniment. I continue my harvest. The piano and the whispered song of the rustling grasses soothe my soul. The beauty of the sunlit hillside is energetic, alive. It dances on the wind. It does not know there is no tomorrow.

From "Prairie Birthday"

The Sand County Almanac, by Aldo Leopold

It is an ordinary graveyard, bordered by the usual spruces, and studded with the usual pink granite or white marble headstones, each with the usual Sunday bouquet of red or pink geraniums. It is extraordinary only in being triangular instead of square, and in harboring, within the sharp angle of its fence, a pin-point remnant of the native prairie on which the graveyard was established in the 1840s. Heretofore unreachable by scythe or mower, this yard-square relic of original Wisconsin gives birth, each July, to a man-high stalk of compass plant or cutleaf Silphium, spangled with saucer-sized yellow blooms resembling sunflowers. It is the sole remnant of this plant along this highway, and perhaps the sole remnant in the western half of our county. What a thousand acres of Silphiums looked like when they tickled the bellies of the buffalo is a question never again to be answered, and perhaps not even to be asked.

This year I found the Silphium in first bloom on 24 July, a week later than usual; during the last six years the average date was 15 July.

When I passed the graveyard again on 3 August, the fence had been removed by a road crew, and the Silphium cut. It is easy now to predict the future; for a few years my Silphium will try in vain to rise above the mowing machine, and then it will die. With it will die the prairie epoch.

Bibliography

Andreas, A. T. *Illustrated Historical Atlas of the State of Iowa.* Chicago: Andreas Atlas Co., 1875.

Andrews, Lorenzo F. *Pioneers of Polk County.* 2 vols. Des Moines: Baker-Trisler Co., 1908.

Bennett, John C. *The History of the Saints; or an Exposé of Joe Smith and Mormonism.* Boston: Leland & Whiting, 1842.

Brown, Leonard. *American Patriotism.* Des Moines: Redhead and Wellslager, 1869.

_____. *American Patriotism.* Reprint. Iowa City: Press of the Camp Pope Bookshop, 2002 .

_____. *Our Own Columbia That is To Be.* Des Moines: E. T. Meredith, 1908.

_____. *Poems of the Prairies.* 3rd ed. Des Moines: Redhead and Wellslager, 1879.

Brigham, Johnson. *Iowa, Its History and Its Foremost Citizens.*

Chicago: The J. S., Clarke Publishing Co., 1918.

Burt, James Wilson. Unpublished family history.

Cook, Lyndon. *The Revelations of the Prophet, Joseph Smith*. Salt Lake City: Deseret Book Co., 1981

Daily State Register. Des Moines.

Des Moines Evening News. Des Moines.

Dixon, J. M. *Centennial History of Polk County, Iowa*. Des Moines: State Register, 1876.

Galland, Isaac. *Galland's Iowa Emigrant*. Chillicothe, OH: Wm. C. Jones, 1840.

Gingerich, Melvin. *The Mennonites in Iowa*. Des Moines: State Historical Society, 1939.

Grigsby, George Washington. Unpublished letters.

Gue, Benjamin F. *History of Iowa: From the Earliest Times to the Beginning of the Twentieth Century*. 4 vols. New York: The Century History Co., 1903.

Hussey, Tacitus. *Beginnings: Reminiscences of Early Des Moines*. Des Moines: American Lithographing and Printing Co., 1919.

Iowa Fish and Fishing. Des Moines: Iowa DNR, 1987.

Iowa Star. Des Moines.

Bibliography

Kearny, Stephen Watts. "Trailmaking on the Frontier." *Palimpsest* 44 (January, 1963): 10–27.

Launius, Roger D. *Joseph Smith III: Pragmatic Prophet.* Urbana, IL: University of Illinois. 1995.

Leopold, Aldo. *The Sand County Almanac.* New York, Oxford University Press, 1949.

Madison Township court records.

Madrid Register News. Madrid, IA.

Noll, Mark A. *A History of Christianity in America and Canada.* Grand Rapids, MI: Wm. B. Eerdmans Publishing Co., 1992.

Polk City Centennial Book. Madrid, IA, 1975.

Polk City Board of Health Records.

Polk City City Council Minutes.

Polk County Medical Society. *History of Medicine in Polk County.* Des Moines: Polk County Medical Society, 1951.

Riley, Glenda. *Frontierswomen: The Iowa Experience.* Ames, IA: Iowa State University Press, 1981.

Rodgers, Mary Schaal. Unpublished family history.

Sanford, Netti. *Early Sketches of Polk County, Iowa.* Newton, IA: Charles A. Clarke, 1874.

Sage, Leland. *A History of Iowa*. Ames, IA: Iowa State University Press, 1974.

Sunday Union. Junction City, KS.

The History of Polk County, Iowa. Des Moines: Union Historical Company, 1880.

Wasp. Nauvoo, IL.

CPSIA information can be obtained
at www.ICGtesting.com
Printed in the USA
LVHW101405230623
750091LV00001B/40